"With *Design Sprint*, Banfield, Lombardo and Wax have created the blueprint for intelligent product design in the 21st century. This power trio of product lays out a groundbreaking new process by which organizations of all sizes can design quickly while also mitigating misfire.*Design Sprint* isn't a book for startups; it's not a book for the Fortune 500; it's a book for every company looking to improve products. Simply put- *Design Sprint* should be on the desk of every professional working in digital products, because I can guarantee you it will soon be on the desks of their competitors."

– Andy Miller,
Chief Innovation Architect at Constant Contact

"I love the Design Sprint method and use it frequently in my work. *Design Sprint* is a concise, practical guide to the technique.»

– Josh Seiden, co-author,
"Lean UX: Applying Lean Principles to Improve User Experience."

"Keeping up with the accelerating pace of innovation requires rethinking how to create successful products. The answer lies in the *Design Sprint*, emphasizing efficiency, effectiveness and organizational buy-in."

– Keith Hopper,
Lecturer in Entrepreneurship at Olin College of Engineering

"Cross-functional collaboration is at the heart of successful product innovation efforts. Design—of products, of processes, of teams and of organizations—is, at its core, a cross-functional practice. This book focuses on bringing elements of the design discipline to a broad swathe of practitioners (not just designers) in a clear, step-by-step way that doesn't intimidate non-designers, but instead motivates them to participate and engage. All of this is in the service of building better products and teams."

– Jeff Gothelf Author,
Lean UX

"Time-to-market is a critical factor in the success of many digital products. With design sprints, you can arrive at the right design, faster. This book provides a clear, easy-to-follow framework that can help your team to implement—and benefit from—design sprints."

– Jorge Arango,
Partner at Futuredraft

design
sprint

A Practical Guidebook for Building Great Digital Products

Richard Banfield, C. Todd Lombardo, and Trace Wax

A Practical Guidebook for Building Great Digital Products

by Richard Banfield, C. Todd Lombardo, and Trace Wax

Copyright © 2016 Richard Banfield, C. Todd Lombardo, and Trace Wax. All rights reserved.
Printed in Canada.

Published by O'Reilly Media, Inc., 1005 Gravenstein Highway North, Sebastopol, CA 95472.

O'Reilly books may be purchased for educational, business, or sales promotional use. Online editions are also available for most titles (*http://safaribooksonline.com*). For more information, contact our corporate/institutional sales department: 800-998-9938 or *corporate@oreilly.com*.

Acquisitions Editor: Nick Lombardi	Indexer: Ron Strauss
Editor: Angela Rufino	Interior Designer: Michael Connors
Production Editor: Nicole Shelby	Cover Designer: Michael Connors
Copyeditor: Jasmine Kwityn	Illustrator: Rebecca Demarest
Proofreader: Kim Cofer	

Printing History

October 2015: First Edition

Revision History for the First Edition

2015-09-18: First Release

See *http://oreilly.com/catalog/errata.csp?isbn=9781491923177* for release details.

The O'Reilly logo is a registered trademark of O'Reilly Media, Inc. *Design Sprint*, the cover image, and related trade dress are trademarks of O'Reilly Media, Inc.

978-1-491-92317-7

[TC]

Table of Contents

Foreword

Why Care About Design Sprints?

These days, few would argue that the pace of change in the business world isn't accelerating—it's generally agreed that every industry faces some kind of disruption in the coming years. This leaves continuous business innovation as the only way to maintain any kind of competitive advantage in the long run.

Innovation in today's connected world doesn't just mean launching new products and services. It also means new business models, which often require different ways of organizing and new forms of organization design.

But most organizations today aren't designed for continuous innovation. Innovation, if it happens at all, happens slowly. Innovation teams must often make do with meager resources as margins shrink in other areas of the business. People in the organization are attached to existing models and ideas. They have formed deeply embedded habits and routines that make it hard to let go of the current mindset or imagine alternatives. If new businesses, or new products and services, make it to launch, there are often problems getting people aligned around new ways of thinking and getting them to take ownership of a new way of working.

Design sprints are an exciting new approach: they get people aligned around new ideas, create more ownership and buy-in, get new ideas to prototype and launch more quickly and efficiently—and with higher quality.

Design sprints create alignment and buy-in because they get more people involved in the design process, working together to co-create new products and prototypes. People are more engaged when they are involved in the creation process.

Design sprints are faster and more efficient because they are "timeboxed," which means they give design teams a way to eliminate distractions, focus their full attention, and get tangible results in short time frames.

Design sprints also increase quality by involving more people from more parts of the organization, including the people who will be tasked with execution and understanding the implementation challenges.

The design sprint is an important new approach and an essential practice for organizations that are serious about innovation. The book you are now holding in your hands was written by pioneers in the field who will guide you, step by step, through this process of running a successful design sprint.

Good luck!

— Dave Gray, coauthor of *Gamestorming* and founder of XPLANE
May 12, 2015, St. Louis, MO

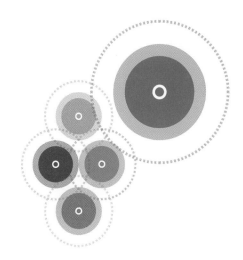

This book is for you.

You're the product person in your organization. You may have no one reporting to you. You might have 50 people in your product group. You might be responsible for the entire product. Maybe the design team doesn't report to you, nor do the developers or marketing and sales teams. Maybe you're in a startup without all those defined roles, and you wear a lot of hats. Maybe you're in a large enterprise organization that has each one defined to the nth degree. Maybe you are a product design freelancer. You might work in an agency as a consultant. You probably have read a blog post about this process. Maybe you even tried one yourself. You're very likely wondering how your unique needs will work with design sprints and are seeking more information than you can find in a few blog posts.

If any of these descriptions sound familiar, then this book was intended for you.

Preface

There were three things that drove us to create this book—in short, we want to:

- Reduce the number of products built that do not add value
- Provide practical applications to the product design and development process for a range of companies
- Improve the accessibility of design sprints

We're attracted to the design sprint process because it's a simple way for prototyping and testing just about any product in a week or less.

Like many product teams, we've witnessed the creation of far too many products that didn't have a good market fit. These misfires waste money and energy—but worst of all, they waste time. For many startups, getting a product to market quickly is the difference between life and death. For enterprises, getting the resources behind the right ideas is critical—otherwise, you launch products customers do not want. Further, in enterprises, the challenge is often more complicated than just time and cash; there's also organizational politics to deal with, as some in large organizations pursue their own agendas.

Might there be a process out there that helps control costs, reduces the waste of going in the wrong direction, and helps keep the peace? Could such a fabled thing exist in the chaotic world of product design?

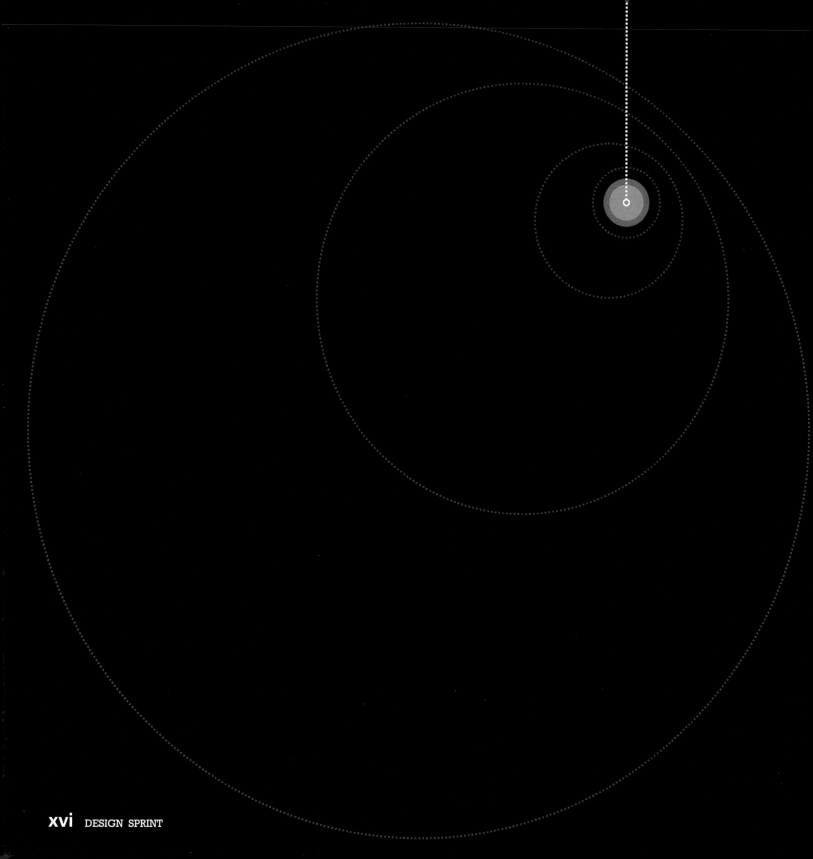

Although digital products have only been with us for a few decades, they have become the dominant way we communicate and consume information. At the time of writing this book, there were 500+ new apps being released into the wild every single day! That doesn't even include the related physical products and services that accompany those apps. At that rate, it's hard to grasp the effort and time needed to make so many products, let alone understand the wasted hours and dollars.

You'd think that digital products would be easier to build than physical products. CEOs and founders often can't understand why their investments in digital products aren't paying off. The path to creating digital products appears so much easier: no injection molding, no flying to China to meet suppliers—hardly a whiff of dirty labor at all. Building a digital product is, in fact, relatively cheap and quick. But building the right product to win in the marketplace is as hard and grueling as ever. This is because the key components to digital products are not pixels and code, but rather people, time, and process. And people are always going to be complicated.

If you're a product lead, time (or lack thereof) is what keeps you up at night. Having collectively worked on over 800 digital products, we feel your pain.

We will focus on the realities of designing digital products, and lay out a practical guide to implementing the design sprint principles and techniques. Knowing full well that there is no single way to create the perfect product, we don't want to sound prescriptive. However, in all cases, having a disciplined and proven process wins out over winging it. This book will help almost anyone working on digital products go from knowledge to action.

Another distinguishing element of this book is that we discuss how design sprints fit into the real world. Unlike in controlled environments or case studies, things don't always align. In the turbulent reality of our lives, it's hard to find five days of uninterrupted time. It's hard to get the attention of the executives. It's hard to find testing subjects who fit your exact target profile. This book was written for the sticky, messy, chaotic world we all live in.

We interviewed dozens of product professionals just like you, and we saw a wide variety in the way design sprints are being used. In fact, no two organizations we spoke with ran them exactly the same way. Google Ventures evangelizes a five-day process, while Intrepid Pursuits does a design sprint over four to six weeks. Agencies like Fresh Tilled Soil have undertaken sprints that take up to two weeks. At the other end of the spectrum, a design sprint can be run in a few hours. But be careful of the desire to shorten it too much! At larger companies like Constant Contact, a design sprint can last from a half day up to nine days, depending on the project. The design sprint is a framework, not a set of rules. We'll show you several ways to tailor a design sprint to meet your specific needs.

As flexible as design sprints are, we like the approach better than most design processes for one simple reason: it's as far from the "gut feeling" approach employed by many product designers as you can get. Patrick Solvabarro, the CEO of Upward Labs, said after going through a design sprint, "These design sprints are a lot like mini science experiments." We like that comparison. The scientific process has successfully given us a model to get our ideas out of our heads (a hypothesis) and test them against the pressures of the big bad world (experimentation) so that we can either validate the hypothesis or figure out what's not working.

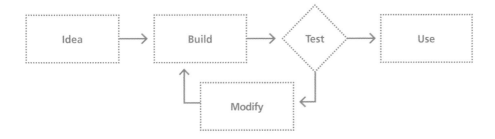

The trial-and-error method (after E. E. Lewis)

Many great scientists, artists, and engineers have built their work on the "ideate, build, test, validate" model. E. E. Lewis, professor emeritus of mechanical engineering at Northwestern University, tells the story of how science and engineering came together to create the technological world of the 21st century in his book *Masters of Technology*. He cites the idea-build-test-use cycle that was likely used by many famous innovators.[1] Galileo was one of the famous innovators to use experimentation to prove his ideas valid or not. As part of a now legendary experiment, he dropped two balls of different materials and weights from the leaning Tower of Pisa, and observed that they landed on the ground at the same time, which was in contrast to the conventional thinking of the time. Edison famously iterated over 300 different designs on his way to inventing the lightbulb. Picasso is considered as one of the most prolific artists, not because he produced many artworks, but because he constantly experimented with artistic directions.

1 E. E. Lewis, *Masterworks of Technology: The Story of Creative Engineering, Architecture, and Design* (Amherst, NY: Prometheus Books, 2004).

We think it's time that product teams did the same.

This process won't prevent failures, but it'll help your team identify them quickly and move you forward to the next breakthrough. There's no process that will prevent mistakes. In addition, we're not looking to eliminate mistakes entirely. Failing faster is a part of the process. The design sprint process gives you "bounce back" power. By providing almost immediate feedback, the design sprint allows you to determine if a proposed direction is likely to lead to failure, and if so, can help you to find the path to success more quickly. You might fail a few times, but you'll have the tools to get back up and tackle the next challenge.

Design sprints are a great way to make sense of the complicated design considerations. Translating the objectives or problem into a narrative and then physically crafting potential solutions is a powerful way to make customer needs and desires visible and visceral. Connecting these customer stories to practical and emotional user feedback via testing generates a road map that becomes the path for future design and development work.

Who This Book Is For

We interviewed CEOs and founders of startups, CTOs, product managers, product owners, VPs of product management, and lead designers. We asked them what worked in their product design cycles, and what didn't. They told us how they structure teams and keep people focused. What we learned is that no two design sprints are exactly alike. We have included their perspectives here so you can learn from varied experiences in driving product development using the design sprint approach.

Very often, the person driving the design sprint won't be a senior executive. If you're a product manager trying to get the CEO, CMO, and key stakeholders to give you up to five dedicated days, you're going to need more than a nice smile. Finding support for a design sprint requires that you communicate the value of the process and outcomes. The three greatest values we often see are the alignment of a team around a product concept, the reduction of resource expenditure, and the validation of an idea from a customer's perspective. By their intense nature, design sprints spur action.

Who Are We to Tell You?

Well, we've been in your shoes. In many senses, we still are! After many years in product management, C. Todd ran the same sequence of activities during his time as a consultant for design-centric organizational change consultancy XPLANE, as well as his consulting agency, CATALYTIC. In his current role as Innovation Architect at Constant Contact's Small Business Innovation Loft (InnoLoft), C. Todd guides both internal Constant Contact teams and InnoLoft startup residents through design sprints to gain clarity, solicit customer input, and define design direction for their products. He has lost count of how many design sprints he's run to date.

Richard leads a team of senior design strategists and personally runs design sprint sessions with his clients at Fresh Tilled Soil. The team works with clients ranging from Fortune 500 corporations such as Intel and Staples, to venture captial–funded startups and emerging businesses. The design and development team at Fresh Tilled Soil has run over 50 sessions using the design sprint approach.

As a Director at thoughtbot, Trace has led the company's NYC office and has attended and facilitated a large number of product design sprints to ensure projects start with enough initial validation. Collectively, designers and developers at thoughtbot have run hundreds of design sprints, and share their experiences in an open source repository on GitHub.[2]

---

2 *https://github.com/thoughtbot/design-sprint*

How We Wrote This Book

A book about design sprints should be written…well, like a design sprint! We had to solve a large, complex problem in a timeboxed manner. Creating a book with the tools you're writing about keeps you very in tune with the benefits and flaws of the methodology. The design sprint forces a concept to become a reality in a few intense days, and this book was born from an equally extraordinary multiday session.

Our initial hypothesis was that product people need a guidebook to design sprints. After all, if we heard rumblings from our peers, partners, and clients, then this would be worth the investigation. We included as many viewpoints as possible from those who manage digital products and/or consult for them, including product managers, product owners, product designers, CEOs, CTOs, and vice presidents. Four intense days of writing produced a prototype draft of the book that we were able to share with our peers. That prototype was the first iteration of the book you are reading today.

After that initial four-day effort, we reviewed, revised, and continued with our interviews. We secured a contract with O'Reilly to bring this knowledge to the masses. Richard and C. Todd even arm-twisted Trace to visit Boston a few times. We wrote, ate, drank, wrote, slept, and wrote some more. We then held remote pair-writing sessions to refine the output and had one final "book sprint" to finish it all off. And really, is it ever finished?

How This Book Is Organized

This book is divided into two parts: the first three chapters cover the basics, including some background information, and the benefits and limitations of design sprints. This part also looks at a few different ways to incorporate a design sprint in your organization by showing many ways we, or others, have implemented them. The next chapters in the second part cover the details of how to run a design sprint yourself, with each chapter outlining the crucial steps from planning to execution to follow up.

Part I, The What, Why, and How of Design Sprints, includes the following chapters:

Chapter 1, What Is a Design Sprint?

Before we get into it, let's define what it is, and talk about where it came from.

Chapter 2, When (and When Not) to Do a Design Sprint

Here we'll review the reasons to do a design sprint (as well as reasons not to do one).

Chapter 3, How to Approach Design Sprints

We'll address the flexibility of this framework by showing you variations on the typical five-day design sprint, including sprints as short as three hours and up to as long as four weeks.

Part II, How to Design Sprint, includes the following chapters:

Chapter 4, Before the Design Sprint: Make a Plan

We'll get you ready to go with topics such as: What information will you need? Who should be there? Where will the design sprint happen? How long should it be?

Chapter 5, Phase 1: Understand

This phase is about identifying and clarifying the problem at hand. You'll get the background on your users and identify their needs and workflows, so that you can set yourself up to create a solution.

Chapter 6, Phase 2: Diverge

Through collaborative brainstorming and sketching exercises, you'll explore a range of possibilities that solve the problem you've identified.

Chapter 7, Phase 3: Converge

You'll distill your large number of ideas into one or two solutions to move forward with and test.

Chapter 8, Phase 4: Prototype

We'll talk about a number of ways to bring your solution to life and get it in front of your users.

Chapter 9, Phase 5: Test

Here's where the rubber meets the road and you test what you've created with people who would use it. We'll talk about how to run your test and interpret the results.

Chapter 10, After the Design Sprint: Capture, Iterate, and Continue

You're done with the design sprint, so what's next? We'll talk about ways to integrate the output and outcome into follow-on workflows such as Agile/Scrum, follow-on design exercises, or other methods.

Acknowledgments

We'd like to thank everyone at O'Reilly: Nick Lombardi for bringing us into the mix, Angela Rufino for editing the heck out of us, Edie Freedman for her design direction, and Dellaena Maliszewski for all her marketing help.

Our technical reviewers, Keith Hopper, Scott Jenson, Harry Max, Joe McNeil, and Dan Saffer, provided critical feedback that was incredibly helpful in shaping this content.

Our colleagues, Alicia Chavero (h2i Institute) and Steven Fisher (NetApp), also commented on a few chapters for us.

The support from our companies was fantastic. Huge thanks to the Fresh Tilled Soil team: Michael Connors for mocking up the design of the book and dealing with C. Todd's numerous cover concepts, Mark Grambau for his mad illustrations, and Chris Wilcox and Alex Stetson for their marketing brilliance.

Thank you to the team at Constant Contact's Small Business Innovation Loft: Andy Miller and Laura Northridge for their support of C. Todd writing this book. Innovation Catalyst Ethan Bagley for his help in reviewing our first prototype, which we made in Northampton. Innovation Catalysts Jill Starett and Kayla Doan, who were a delight to train how to run design sprints. Training Jill, Kayla, and Ethan was a big help in refining the methodology, because when you have to teach something, you must know it inside out. From Constant Contact's User Experience team: Damon Dimmock for his wisdom on how design sprints integrate with Agile. Michael Kennedy, Cay Lodine, Tom Gallo, Sam Roach, and Scott Williams for being amazing designers and researchers who participated in many design sprints. From the Constant Contact corporate team: Erika Tower for her help in navigating the internal public relations and investor relations, Jason Fidler for his help with external public relations. And finally, Vice President of Product, Piyum Samaraweera, and Senior Vice President of Product, Ken Surdan, for their willingness to embrace new ways of approaching product design and development.

Many thanks to thoughtbot's entire design team for championing the design sprint concept, for performing so many design sprints, and for sharing your knowledge with us and with the community. A big thank you to Galen Frechette for creating and blogging about our design sprint approach, Dan Croak for distilling that and placing it front and center in thoughtbot's playbook, Alex Baldwin for his thoughtful history of the design sprint approach, and Andrew Cohen and Corwin Harrell for a shining example of how to iterate to turn things around when users didn't want the first thing we came up with. A special thanks to Kyle Fiedler who distilled and open sourced our methodology so people can follow it to do their own design sprints. A big thank you as well to our clients who shared their stories and materials, especially Character Lab, whose well-run design sprint turned into a big win.

To all the people we interviewed, thank you so much for your time, willingness to be interviewed, and for sharing your experience with us:

Matt Bridges at Intrepid
Heather Abbott at Nasdaq
Steve Fisher at NetApp
Patrick Solvabarro at Upward Labs
Marc Guy at Faze-1
Scott Jangro at Shareist
Damon Dimmick at Constant Contact
Brian Colcord at LogMeIn

Dana Mitroff-Silvers

Karen Cross and Jurgen Spangl at Atlassian

Larissa Chavarría at The Advisory Board

Rie Yamaoka at Truila

Alex Britez at MacMillan Education

Dan Ramsden at BBC

Alok Jain at 3 Pillar Global

Seth Godin

Ben Ronning at Tradecraft

Andrew McCarthy at Red Radix

Alan Klement at ReWired

Alex Nemeroff at Dynamo

Ariadna Font Llitjos at IBM

Finally, we're hugely appreciative of our families and significant others. Without your love and support, this book would have never happened.

And finally finally, we'd like to thank the Academy. We don't exactly know who or what this Academy is, but we hear them thanked all the time. So thank you, Academy!

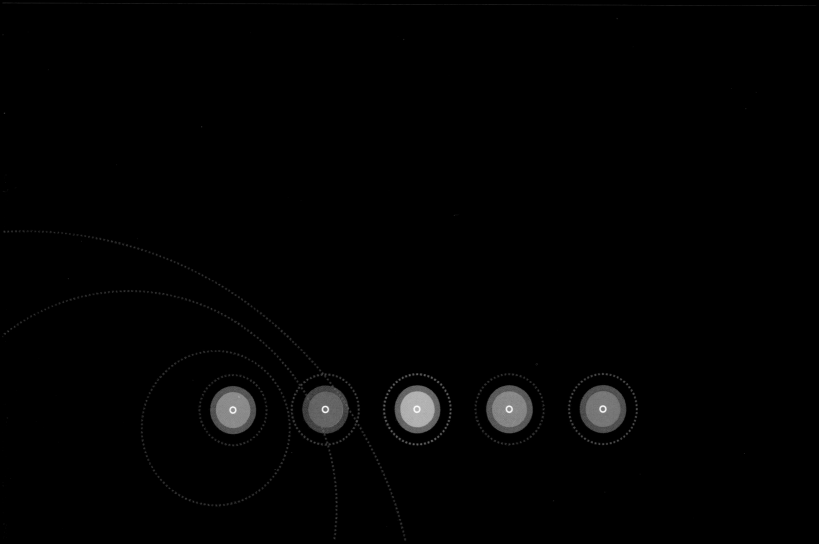

The What, Why, and How of Design Sprints

The chapters in this part explain what a design sprint is and why the current approach to design might not work for today's product designers. We'll take a look at challenges with existing design paths and compare them to design sprints. There is no one-size-fits-all design process, but a design sprint can adapt to meet the needs of many projects. Specifically, we'll look at the ways you and your team can benefit from running a design sprint for your current projects to increase the opportunity for a positive outcome. You'll hear from design leaders about their experiences and how they have used this flexible approach to increase productivity and reduce the risks associated with product design. By the end of this part, we'll have lifted the veil on this relatively new process to give you a better understanding of what makes a design sprint work.

Chapter 1

What Is a Design Sprint?

A design sprint is a flexible product design framework that serves to maximize the chances of making something people want. It is an intense effort conducted by a small team where the results will set the direction for a product or service.

A design sprint consists of five discrete phases:

0. Prepare (Get ready)
1. **Understand (review background and user insights)**
2. **Diverge (brainstorm what's possible)**
3. **Converge (rank solutions, pick one)**
4. **Prototype (create a minimum viable concept)**
5. **Test (observe what's effective for users)**
6. Iterate...to another design sprint, or a Lean and Agile build process such as Scrum or Continuous Delivery/Extreme Programming

A design sprint reduces the risk of downstream mistakes and generates vision-led goals the team can use to measure its success. For the purposes of this book, we'll focus on digital products, as our direct experience lies in that arena, though the design sprint has roots in gaming and architecture,[1] and many industries have employed them successfully.

Uses of a Design Sprint

There are many ways to utilize a design sprint; one way is to look at which stage of development the project is in. Are you at the beginning and need to understand a wide array of unknowns? Or are you looking at a mature product that has been on the market for a while?

At the beginning of a project

You might use a design sprint to initiate a change in process or start the innovation of a product concept. This works well when you're exploring opportunities with the goal of coming up with original concepts that ultimately will be tested in the real world—for example, if we need to understand how young parents would buy healthcare products online.

In the middle of a project

You might use a design sprint to start a new cycle of updates, expanding on an existing concept or exploring new ways to use an existing product. For example, we worked with a marketing data company that realized the data it gathered might be useful to other market segments. Building a prototype gave the team the validation it needed and prompted a deeper investment into that product segment, which ultimately was rewarded with a significant increase in sales.

---

1 *http://alexbaldwin.com/qcon-2014/*

For a mature project

A design sprint can also be used to test a single feature or subcomponent of a product. This allows you to focus on a particular aspect of the design. For example, your team might need to know what improvements can be made to the onboarding process. Using the design sprint to discover the pros and cons of a new onboarding channel could give you granular insights into a high-return part of the product experience.

However you use it, the design sprint brings clarity to your road map to kickstart and obtain initial validation for almost any new, product design–related work.

How the Design Sprint Came to Be

The design sprint evolved from a number of different approaches to design. As Agile and design thinking became more popular, design sprints became a way to encapsulate them.

From Agile

The word *sprint* comes from the world of Agile, and it describes a short period of time, typically 1–4 weeks, set aside to accomplish a focused goal. The design sprint is no different. It uses the original concept of the sprint to describe a period of time dedicated to working on the necessary design thinking. This time-bounded paradigm is critical to the success of the design sprint. *Timeboxing*, as it's sometimes called, is essential to driving the right types of behavior from the participants. In addition to speeding up the product design and development process, it also takes advantage of core parts of our human nature: energy economy and social collaboration.

From design charrettes

Going way back, the term *charrette* was used to describe any collaborative workshop session among designers, and design-thinking frameworks from Stanford's d.school emerged as a way to apply more structure to this concept. Industrial product design firms like IDEO developed short-cycle design sessions called deep dives, which built on the design charrette concept popularized by Stanford's d.school.

IDEO's most famous example is the Shopping Cart Concept, a deep dive that was featured on *Nightline* in 1999.[2] The team pushed back on age-old mythologies about how design gets done and brought a multidisciplinary team together to brainstorm, research, prototype, and obtain user feedback that went from idea to a working model in four days. By collapsing the time constraints, the designers were essentially holding a gun to their heads and forcing themselves to come up with better solutions in less time.

From digital product design

The influence of industrial design and software design was the genesis, but it was the emergence of digital product design that brought on a more formal framework for testing ideas out in the wild. Several organizations started to converge upon similar processes with similarly named phases.

From Google Ventures

Although there have been company-specific versions of this approach used over the last decade, it was the work of Jake Knapp at Google Ventures (GV) that brought them to a broader audience.

GV invests in startups, and at times those startups require product design advice to align their teams. To help with this, GV would send a designer to work with each startup for one week's time. As it turns out, these processes have five phases, one for each day of that week. The structure and time constraint proved useful. Lo and behold, the design sprint was born.

---

2 *http://www.ideo.com/work/shopping-cart-concept*

Created for Startups, Great for Enterprises

For startups

Startups are notoriously fast-moving environments that value speed to market over almost everything else. This commitment to speed gives them an advantage but also risks leaving out a lot of the essential thinking and testing required to build a truly useful product. Too many products go to market without customer validation. How do you maintain the speed while including the necessary research and design thinking? Many startups in the Constant Contact InnoLoft Program cite a design sprint as one of the most valuable parts of their participation.

For enterprises

Enterprises that have well-established processes may also look to a design sprint as a way to accelerate their product design and development so that they can work more like a fast-moving startup. The accelerated learning can give the enterprise an advantage and also reduce the amount of resource investments for exploration of product ideas and concepts. Spending three to five days on a project idea to see if it makes sense to move forward is better than working three to five months, only to discover it would have been better to not have proceeded at all.

Any product or product feature will be validated or invalidated. You can do that validation yourself, or let the market do it. Which do you think will be less expensive?

Success = Time and Money Saved + Minds Blown

A design sprint's success can be measured in many ways. What works for metrics in your organization may differ from others. Here are a few ways we have seen design sprints measured.

Success by preventing failure

You can't change what you can't measure, right? One of the biggest questions we initially faced when implementing design sprints in our organizations was "How do you measure the success of a design sprint?" In our experience, it was often the absence of something that we were trying to measure. For example, how do you measure the amount of time you won't spend on bad product development? How much money will you save by not investing in a product that will make less ROI? Those questions point toward future gains by not spending some difficult-to-calculate amount of time or money. How do you measure the absence of a failed product?

There's no way you're not going to save yourself time and money. Because the way these deals usually work is to go out and build things and just invest thousands of dollars and all this time, and then, find out that it falls flat. There is no testing done, no exploration done with end users," remarked Dana Mitrof-Silvers, a design-thinking consultant who works with many nonprofits, such as the Indianapolis Museum of Art and the Denver Museum of Nature and Science. She measures the success of a design sprint by the ideas generated. "While ideas aren't usually the problem, most organizations find themselves with an excess of ideas—validated ideas and the execution is what's missing.

When you get validation

In many cases, a design sprint will lead you to something that gets initial user validation, where the next steps are defined. You'll have reduced risk by doing some validation early, and developed next steps faster than would have otherwise been possible. Character Lab[3] had a design sprint like this with thoughtbot. In a week, a large group of diverse stakeholders from an educational nonprofit got on the same page about what would be built, and remarked upon how quickly they reached agreement.

3 *https://characterlab.org/character-growth-card*

Teachers and students were excited about the prototype they saw and couldn't wait to use it. What we needed to build was clear and could proceed unimpeded at a good clip, which was very much needed given the size of the app and its shoestring, nonprofit budget.

Some validation, some things to fix

Sometimes issues come to light that need some clear changes in your product, and you can fix those things and plan additional research. For example, thoughtbot did a design sprint for Tile[4] to optimize the team's mobile app design to help users find keys with a device attached. After the sprint, we iterated based on what we learned and continued additional research sessions. In those following weeks, we found that making the device beep louder helped users find keys three times faster than anything else.

When you don't get validation

Design sprints can help prevent you from building the wrong thing even when your customers say it's the right thing. Larissa Levine, from the Advisory Board Company, believes that a design sprint is successful if it guides you toward building the right product feature. As she explains, "Product marketing wants to sell this one feature and says, 'let's build XYZ because we heard that the user said they wanted XYZ,' when actually, that's not the problem at all. They think they want XYZ, but it's not it at all. So you end up building the wrong thing."

Sometimes a design sprint can get rid of those preconceived notions. Michael Webb, cofounder of InnoLoft startup resident itsgr82bme, entered a design sprint with a clear idea in his head about using APIs as a means for connecting its calendar of family-friendly events with other sites' event listings. During the sprint, he realized

---

4 *https://thoughtbot.com/work/tile*

this could be done without using any APIs at all. He ended the sprint in a very different place.

Lastly, a design sprint can stop you from building any product at all. Marc Guy, CEO of Faze1, also went through a design sprint at the InnoLoft. The sprint made him realize his company needed to stop building a product and instead go out and talk to customers. Mind blown, product invalidated! The business model has shifted significantly since then, as it subsequently focused on customer development. In fact, C. Todd didn't see Marc or his team in the InnoLoft much after their design sprint. They were all out talking to customers, even their development team! The results were impressive and yielded an 8x increase in booked revenue over their previous year.

Each design sprint will have its own needs and idiosyncrasies, and you'll have to determine up front what's best for your project. Any good design-thinking process might help identify the real problem in each of these cases. What makes the design sprint approach more effective is the structured, time-constrained framework, along with the appropriate exercises. This will force the team to make decisions and validate ideas faster than most methodologies.

Takeaways:

- A design sprint has five phases: Understand, Diverge, Converge, Prototype, and Test. The names of these phases may vary from company to company, but the overall ethos remains the same: a timeboxed design cycle completed in a collaborative fashion with real user input.

- The focus of a design sprint is to get the validation needed to maximize the chances of creating something people want.

- The process is very flexible and can adapt to different teams and needs.

- Design sprints can be measured in different ways, from number of "good" ideas generated, team alignment, company direction, and even halting a project.

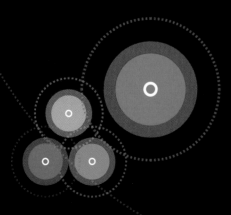

Chapter 2

When (and When Not) to Do a Design Sprint

In this chapter, we explore why design sprints make sense for product design work. As risk is an inherent part of any project, we'll discuss why design sprints can improve your chances for success and reduce your risk of failure. This management of project risk also extends to how you align your team and the outcomes. This chapter describes ways to get everyone on the same page, even when you have a team made up of several diverse representatives. We'll also discuss when a design sprint isn't your best option. As we've said before, there is no magic wand in the design process, so it's important to know when not to use these techniques and approaches. When projects lack a purpose or a raison d'être, they can be doomed to failure, even when you have a solid framework like the design sprint.

Why Do a Design Sprint?

To be successful in creating digital products, you must reduce your risk of failure, but it's nearly impossible to eliminate risk completely. Traditionally, design leads have tried planning their way out of that conundrum, only to find that no amount of planning can guarantee an outcome. Our gray hairs stand testimony to the failure of Waterfall and even Agile project management. To maximize the chances of building something people want, we need to create the most minimal way to test that without expending too many resources.

At Constant Contact, C. Todd facilitated a four-day design sprint for the mobile team with a premise to include the wealth of Constant Contact's helpful resources and tips for crafting great emails in an elegant mobile app. "Helpful information all at your fingertips," was the premise. During the Test phase, all six participants said something to the effect of "That looks nice, but I will never use it." While we may have been disappointed with that result, it allowed us to divert our time, energy, and resources into building a mobile app our customers would actually value.

Speed, efficiency, and focus will increase

With the environmental pressure of a clear drop-dead schedule, your brain jumps into action. The pressure created by the short time frame jump-starts your brain and your body's physiology to produce more of the molecules we need to create solutions. Research shows that these hard deadlines push us into a state of flow.[1]

The time constraints will also cause you to look at things from a new perspective. As Joshua Brewer notes in *52 Weeks of UX*, "The imposition of constraints can lead to

---

1 This happens when you move from a stressful state to a state known as flow (aka getting into the zone), as famously described by Mihaly Csikszentmihalyi in *Flow: The Psychology of Optimal Experience* (New York: Harper Perennial Modern Classics, 2008 [1990]).

great design decisions. Limitations often force you to view things from a perspective you are not accustomed to and, in turn, can stimulate the clarity and purpose of the design, rather than debilitate and hinder your creative process."[2]

To align a diverse team

A design sprint is a highly collaborative process designed to enable each participant's voice to be heard. Structured individual work, planned group discussions, and a clear diverge and converge process will guide a team to get on the same page around the artifacts it produces together. There's a well-studied phenomenon called the "co-creation effect," which shows that when organizations and consumers create a product or service together, both parties will have a greater interest in the outcome.[3,4] The same can apply to your team as you work through the design sprint.

The state of flow that the participants enjoy together will make them bond with one another. To quote Steven Kotler, an author who writes about this flow state,[5] "the key message here is that organizations that are interested in these kinds of high-performing, flow-bonded, tight teams must absolutely allow those teams the space to take risks. Companies lacking that Silicon Valley 'fail frequently, fail faster, fail forward' motto are denying their workforce the easy access to flow that risk provides and the incredibly important social bonds that result."

---

2 Joshua Brewer, "Constraints Fuel Creativity," 52 Weeks of UX, *http://bit.ly/52wks-CFC.*

3 Anne Roggeveen, Michael Tsiros, and Dhruv Grewal, "The 'Co-Creation Effect:' The Impact of Using Co-Creation as a Service Recovery Strategy," *Babson Faculty Research Fund Working Papers,* paper 41 (2009).

4 Michael I. Norton, Daniel Mochon, and Dan Ariely, "The IKEA Effect: When Labor Leads to Love," *Journal of Consumer Psychology* Vol. 22, No. 3 (July 2012): 453-460.

5 Steven Kotler, *The Rise of Superman: Decoding the Science of Ultimate Human Performance* (New York: Houghton Mifflin, 2014).

To have a clear process

As designers and developers of digital products, we love a good process with a clear set of steps to follow. The design sprint process structures the right initial things to do, which is beneficial especially when a new team is coming together to start a new effort and many things haven't yet been defined. Following the steps defined in this framework, the team will work along a proven path through the essential conversations required when beginning a new effort.

To start a new project in a clear direction

When a new project starts, the team involved needs to know how to begin and how to proceed. A design sprint will leave you with a direction, user definition, user journey, and prototype, which if validated provides a great place for design and development to start. The aspects that aren't validated will provide a list of questions to pursue and issues to resolve.

This can help with creating an initial estimate and assessment of technical feasibility. The artifacts and discoveries from a design sprint can be used to create the first prioritized list of things to design and implement. There will still be plenty of new information, changes, and details as the project proceeds, but you can hit the ground running.

When we interviewed Matt Bridges, CTO at Intrepid Labs, and asked whether he's seen a difference between projects that began with a design sprint and projects that did not, he replied, "The last two weeks are less crazy!" The clear direction that was set initially meant that things were finished earlier.

When Not to Use a Design Sprint

A design sprint isn't a magic bullet to address every need and situation. There are times where a design sprint isn't the right course of action in a project, though it might be later. The following sections detail some instances in which you would not want to do a design sprint.

The product is already very well-defined

Some new efforts don't require much design thinking. For example, there might already be a validated design that's already been agreed to. A design sprint also wouldn't suit a reimplementation of existing functionality where there isn't an opportunity for exploring improvements, reductions, or changes.

Significant research is needed beyond the scope of 1–2 days of interviews

We've learned that a design sprint needs to have some inputs and most often that is some form of data. We'll get into detail in Chapters 4 and 5, but if you lack any user/customer research data, it will be difficult to get all of it in one or two days. There are two possible options: you can extend the sprint or alternatively, you can focus it on research only, forgoing testing and instead digging into the customer's needs and problems. "Get out of the building" is a phrase Steve Blank evangelizes to his entrepreneurship students, and this applies to product people in larger organizations as well.

The project is only a few days in scope

A design sprint is typically a five-day effort, give or take. If you only have a few days to get something released, it won't make sense to spend all of your time on a design sprint. You can, however, perform a few key design sprint exercises at the beginning, to get off to a good start.

In Chapter 3, we'll address in detail the different time scales we have come across during the course of our research.

The business opportunity isn't clear

Design sprints are excellent at helping bring clarity around a potential direction, but they cannot see through the densest of fog. There needs to be a good enough general sense that the effort you're beginning will add enough value. There needs to be a business case for a possible solution to the problem area you're approaching.

The scope is far too broad

You don't need to know many specifics before beginning a design sprint, but you'll want to know the general problem area before you get started. A design sprint that tries to bite off more than it can chew may result in a lowest common denominator solution that may not fit the initial problem the sprint defined. As much as we like silver bullets, they are like unicorns and do not truly exist or function as we desire.

A more sophisticated product development effort is required

A design sprint is the beginning of a conversation about a product, not the end of one.

What is produced will still need to be developed further. A design sprint is not a method for getting a more sophisticated product development effort done for less money and time. However, we have seen people fall into this trap, no matter how much expectation setting we put forth at the beginning of the project.

You won't break up with your idea: The IKEA effect

The IKEA effect is when participants fall in love with an idea simply because they exerted some level of effort in creating it. The design sprint can be a mechanism for letting go, as sometimes users will tell you things you don't want to hear, but if there's an unwillingness to accept a change in direction, a design sprint won't help. There should be a 1-800 helpline for that.

Takeaways:

- A design sprint is useful when you need to reduce the risk of failure, gain efficiency, align a team, establish an initial process, or set the direction on a new effort.

- A design sprint is less useful in the following cases: when a product is already well defined, if significant additional research is needed, if the allotted time is too short, or if a business opportunity isn't clear.

- A design sprint cannot accomplish everything, so scope appropriately. It is not a substitute for complex product development, nor if there's an unwillingness in your organization for a change in direction.

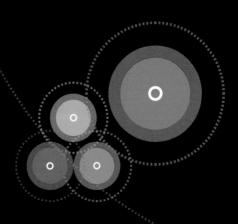

1. UNDERSTAND

2. DIVERGE

3. CONVERGE

4. PROTOTYPE

10:00

Check in.

LEEOR
NURIA
JACEK
DAN
TOM

09:30 START
LEEOR PRESENTS
CLUSTERED
STORIES.
SIMPLIFY +
WRITE UP.

ALEX
NURIA
MARK
(LEEOR)
TOM

JACEK
TOM
DAN.

(-11)

10:00

EX JACEK DON
NURIA
MARK
DOM

10:00

MARK JA
DOM TIM
ALEX (@5)

10:30 TOM

KEEP
STOP
START.

10:15

REVIEW OF
UNDERSTAND
DAY

DOT VOTING
OF SCENARIOS.
WHICH IS
RICHEST?

CUT-OFF
FEEDBACK
+
ANALYSE

IN

11:00

Review
Sprint

JACEK

Feedback

10:30

JOURNEYS
TO
HMWS

GROUP MIND
MAP OF INITIAL
THOUGHTS.

10:00
-
10:15

DIVIDE +
CONQUER.

LEEOR

Revisit
Map.

Review
of Litecycles

Lifecycles

11:00

CREATE

+
MAKE 2ND
iPAD

12:00

Define
Sprint 3
Focus

HMW?
Mindmap.

POST-IT
STORY
BOARD

11:00

CRAZY '8'
IDEAS
BRAINSTORM

IDEATE

11:00

11:45

Chapter 3

How to Approach Design Sprints

You might be wondering if a design sprint will be good for your particular project. Having been in the product design trenches just like you, we know that there are huge benefits to this process, but it's not for everyone and not for every project. We've seen firsthand on hundreds of projects that this focused effort will help you make significant progress in your project in a very short period of time. We also know it has limitations, and we'll talk about that toward the end of this chapter. Let's face it: you will not build Facebook in one design sprint, but you might build a great prototype for a key use case of a social network. However, there may be ideas about products and product features that need vetting before resources can be assigned to help them move forward. Design sprints can also help to create minimum viable products (MVPs). Other projects, such as marketing campaigns, finance initiatives, or even training and support initiatives, could benefit from a design sprint before expending too many resources on a project.

What's the Best Application of Design Sprints?

Design sprints can be used in a variety of ways to develop your product. We'll walk you through a few different ways we have used them or have seen others use them.

A wide variety of projects and people

Brian Colcord, Director, UX and Product Design, at the publicly traded LogMeIn, got the same kick out of discovering design sprints that we had:

"The design sprint was an eye-opening thing to me, because you always struggle within these corporate settings with opinions, and stakeholders, and all of those types of things. When I got introduced to the design sprint, that showed me that you can involve all of these people in that process, and the outcome can be exponentially better and faster than how we were going about it currently. It just really opened my eyes."

The types of projects a design sprint can handle vary. At Constant Contact, C. Todd and his team have run them on a variety of initiatives beyond digital products. The finance team was keen on digging into hypotheses-driven test approaches, the sales and marketing teams were interested in exploring the design and packaging of the product offering, and the franchise team wanted to test different combinations for particular audiences.

As we discussed in the previous chapter, our brains need environmental and internal triggers to get us into the creative flow. To ensure our survival during times when calories needed for creative thinking were not as close as the vending machine, we evolved brains that conserve energy. Your brain wants to hang on to its calories for as long as possible. In times of need, your brain jumps into action and chews on all that stored energy as quickly as possible. Times of need can be artificially manufactured by creating deadlines. Our brain doesn't know the difference. When you create deadlines, your brain stops procrastinating and gives you what you need.

A framework for timeboxed activities

The same thing happens when you create a time-bound design sprint. Scheduled activities and consequences snap your brain into action. The best way to create urgency and get the juices flowing is to set hard dates for the sprint. There is a real need to create extrinsic motivators to get the best results. For example, schedule customer interviews, which will provide the feedback you'll need, on the last day of the sprint or set up a presentation to your bosses to show them what the sprint uncovered. These motivators get you focused, which the brain likes, and forces you to get the really important stuff (e.g., prototyping) completed, so you won't look unprepared come testing day.

Having said this, there is a deliberate and almost paradoxical tension that must be created for this collaboration to be successful. The design sprint is a framework that aims to provide enough structure to get the team engaged and excited while also remaining flexible enough that it doesn't smother the creative process. We'll dive into when to be flexible and when to be structured throughout the book. Time spent with the team needs to be sensitive to the very real technical challenges of building a functional prototype, while supporting the sparks of insight that come from collaborative exploration. The brilliant pianist Bill Evans said it best in his liner notes to Miles Davis's *Kind of Blue*: "Group improvisation is a further challenge. Aside from the weighty technical problem of collective coherent thinking, there is the very human, even social need for sympathy from all members to bend for the common result."

The Ideal Design Sprint: Five Days

A full design cycle in one week

While we've seen design sprints as short as a few hours and as long as a few weeks, our recommendation is to dedicate at least one full day for each of the five phases of the design sprint. Although it's very possible to complete the entire process in three days, we must stress that in no case should you leave out the customer feedback phase. Forgoing this feedback can undermine the very reason you are doing this exercise—to get insights that lead to a better understanding. The ideal design sprint provides time for team members to reflect on their ideas and challenges and also provides opportunities to validate or disrupt those ideas. By allocating a day to each phase, you have time to test assumptions and overcome the possibility of jumping to conclusions. This gives the team the opportunity to reflect on some of the decisions and discussions of the previous days' work. We'll discuss the details of that in the next chapter. In our experience and through the interviews we conducted, we discovered other time frames in which design teams are applying the design sprint framework.

What if you don't have five days? Or you do, but the folks on your team do not, because they have day jobs working on something besides your shiny new project? Yes, everyone has something else to work on. When this happens, you can try some or all of the approaches covered in the following sections—these alternatives are proven to work.

Alternative Approach #1: Compact It

"I can't give you five days. I can give you two."

The biggest challenge to the five-day sprint comes in larger, enterprise organizations. It is difficult to get all the right stakeholders in one place for five uninterrupted days, as many stakeholders have other responsibilities and "day jobs" to attend to.

For many design sprints, the full team only needs to be present for the Understand, Diverge, and Converge phases of the sprint. For the Prototype phase, the participation of the full team is useful to provide the right copy, and it's also useful for everyone to observe the user sessions during the Test phase. However, if it's not possible for everyone to attend, this can be handled by a smaller team. The full team can get the user feedback during a final session once the user testing is complete. That can save two full days of the participants' time.

Even three days is sometimes difficult, so the first three phases can be condensed into two days with the full team. Then the Prototype and Test phases can extend by up to half a day to a full day each, which can make them go at a more relaxed pace.

Alternative Approach #2: Shorten the Days

"I can give you five to six hours each day"

At Constant Contact, C. Todd found through experimentation that a 10 a.m. to 4 p.m. time frame helps alleviate the concerns of having to give up multiple full days to a design sprint. At one point, he tried breaking up the sprint even further into small one and a half to two-hour workshops over the course of two to three months. Some of the participants had many other responsibilities and their schedules were tightly booked. While these design sprints made an impact, their value would have been greater had they been more condensed and not drawn out over multiple months. We abandoned that practice and will now run a workshop but will not engage a full-on design sprint over such a great length of time. There's something magical about the forced intensity a design sprint brings.

Beware of too short

Shortened days do help with alleviating the exasperated response of: "You want me to give you three to five days, are you nuts?!" However, design does take time, and any problem worth solving needs adequate time to be solved.

Alternative Approach #3: Spread It Out

"Let's do bite-sized chunks over four weeks."

Matt Bridges, CTO of Intrepid Labs, a digital design agency focused on mobile app design, told us that his company spreads design sprints over four to six weeks, and for good reason. The agency's team and clients don't have the luxury of getting together for five full consecutive days

Steve Fisher, currently Director of User Experience at NetApp, describes his experience when he worked as UX Director for SeaChange:

"Traditional design sprints in the Google Ventures mode of five days, all day, that's wonderful. If you're a startup funded by Google Ventures, and you need your series A, you're going to be there. But [when] you have 10 other things to do and people to manage, it's hard. You can't do all-day sessions. So we broke them up into two-hour chunks. Get them in the morning because their brains are fresh, 10:00 a.m. to 12:00 p.m., then you wrap up. We did that actually two days a week. We spread it out over a four-week sprint every Tuesday and Thursday. That was the easiest way to do it. We found Tuesday and Thursday, 10:00 a.m. to 12:00 p.m., were optimal times to get people engaged."

Steve clarified that the designers worked on the project for more than just the two hours, and that only during those two-hour sessions were the other cross-functional stakeholders working on specific exercises with the UX team.

Jürgen Spangl at Atlassian had a similar experience when he tried to run a seven-week design sprint. Yes, that's correct, a seven-week design sprint. When we heard that, we thought: that's not a sprint, that's a marathon! "I would never run the seven-week one like how I ran it in the past. As ambitious as it was, it probably had a lot of change. It brought a lot of change in the company trying to skill-up and educate too many people at the same time and all that drawing to an outcome is just not possible."

The danger of this approach is that it essentially becomes like a Waterfall process and the "sprint" is no longer a sprint, rather a leisurely pace.

Alex Britez at MacMillan Education started with a six-day design sprint in his organization, using the following phases:

- **Understanding** Align on the problems to solve
- **Empathy** Bring in stakeholders (students) and interview them
- **Ideation** Categorize insights and generate solutions
- **Decision** Decide which solutions to build and test, by using a science fair–like arena
- **Prototyping** Build the idea into a clickable product
- **Testing** Solicit feedback on the prototype from users

Two key differences in this flavor are an entire day devoted to customer interviewing for empathy, and allowing a prototype build over a weekend to be ready for Monday's testing.

Alternative Approach #4: Ultra-Compact It: A Few Hours

"I can give you a few hours. What can we get done?"

We've sometimes seen projects that can benefit from aspects of the design sprint process, but the entire project is just one week. We can't spend the whole week on design thinking! Or sometimes the stakeholders are available for just a few hours on a larger project.

In cases like these, the sprint can be focused into the essence of the most important aspects. We don't have as much time to diverge and converge as we'd like, but we can still create a concise challenge statement, understand our goals and assumptions, and understand who the users are and what their journey is through what we might want to create for them. After some quick sketching and storyboarding, high-level wireframes can then be reviewed with users and can form the start of a backlog of things to implement, to get a project off to the right start.

In March 2015, this happened at thoughtbot. Peter Bell from Ronin Labs had three weeks to build a new system to run a course for enterprise training. We wanted to begin with a design sprint, but Peter needed to get on a plane in three hours, so that's all the time we had. Three hours? Yes. So off they went and did the quick exercises just described. The result? Peter's now secured seed funding and has the customers and users he needs, starting from nothing.

"One of the other things that we've really done, which is kind of an adaptation of the design sprint is design studios, which I've learned a lot about in the last couple of years. I put them into practice here, and they are more like day-long design sprints, where you kind of have these three design threads and you break off into teams. They allow for including more people, and I think they work better for something that's just like trying to iron out a specific flow, or that's a little bit less of a problem. Design sprints, I think, lend themselves better to bigger, overarching problems. If you're just trying to figure out how we get somebody through a purchase flow or something like that, the design studio day helps to ignite that and push that along. We practice those as well; we use those."

—Brian Colcord, LogMeIn

Alternative Approach #5: Align with Your Team's Agile/Scrum

"My engineering team follows Agile, how can this work together?"

Damon Dimmick at Constant Contact reflected on what he referred to as the "scrumification" of design sprints:

"I basically advocate for a model where, in the Scrum world, the first week before we even get to doing any kind of a design sprint, or even it could be weeks before, we've got a product owner with a backlog and the team is getting together, continuous grooming efforts and the hypotheses are going on that backlog, the assumptions are going on that backlog. This is what is basically called a discovery phase."

He continued on about how the hypotheses drive the work: *"As you get these hypotheses and validations that you want to actually work through, what you're hoping to do is take these into sprints of work, unpack them, understand them, and then the output is actionable stories, which could include designs or they might not, depending on what's needed.*

Once you've got a whole backlog of those, you go through the usual Scrum mechanics, the PO starts to look at their prioritization," and then the team adjusts accordingly.

Match the design sprint length to the Scrum length

Trace and his team at thoughtbot run one-week design sprints, and for some teams at Constant Contact that's also true. Alok Jain, Senior Manager of User Experience Design at 3-Pillar Global, runs two-week design sprints for similar reasons, as his development team runs the Scrum in two-week cycles.

Regardless of the format you ultimately work with, there are many ways to adapt a design sprint to your constraints. The examples given here hopefully offer you a taste of how it may fit into your organization.

Takeaways:

- Timeboxing your efforts creates a sense of urgency. Really: you get stuff done.

- We don't know if there is a limit on how many projects a team can work on, but from our observations it follows that a team focused on one project can be more productive than a team focused on many projects.

- The five phases of a design sprint can sometimes be condensed into a smaller time frame or, alternatively, extended beyond one week—experiment to find which works best in your organization.

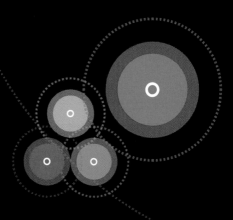

BACKGROUND

✓ RULES
✓ PARKING LOT
✓ AGENDA
✓ PITCH PRACTICE
✓ REVIEW PAST WORK / RESEARCH

GET INSPIRED

✓ GOALS + ANTI GOALS
✓ EXISTING PRODUCT, COMPETITORS + SUBS
✓ FACTS + ASSUMPTIONS

DEFINE the PROBLEM

✓ PROBLEM STATEMENT
CHALLENGE MAPS

DAY 2

GEAR UP
✓ REVIEW AGENDA + BACKGROUND
✓ PITCH PRACTICE
✓ JOB STORIES

GENERATE SOLN'S (2x)
✓ MIND MAP
✓ 8-UP / 6-UP
✓ STORY BOARD
✓ SILENT CRIT / DOT VOTE
✓ GROUP CRITIQUE
~~INDIVIDUAL WIREFRAME~~

WRAP-UP

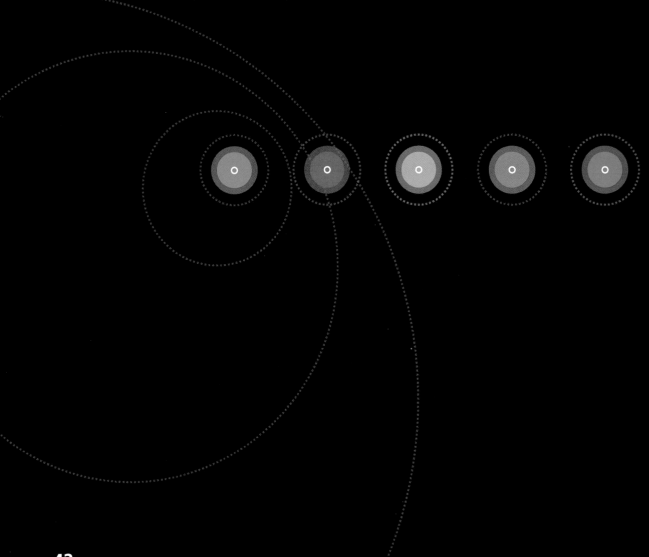

How to
Design Sprint

What's next is a walk through the specifics of the timing, logistics, and project management of running a design sprint for your team, project, or company. We'll guide you through scoping, team recruiting and selection, space preparation, and all the details that make this a truly engaging experience. You'll learn how to run a design sprint with confidence and you'll learn from our collective experience.

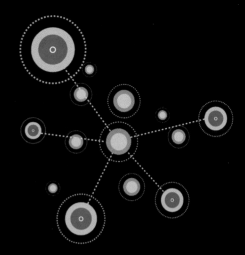

Diverge

Generate ideas to
solve that problem

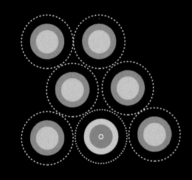

Understand

Define and unpack
the problem to solve

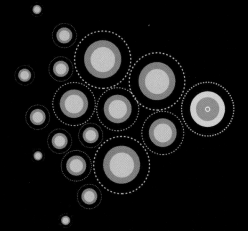

Converge

Decide which ideas to
pursue for testing

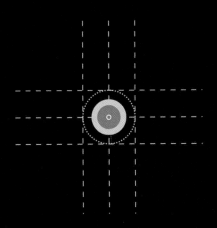

Prototype

Build a prototype
users can play with

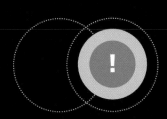

Test

Validate your assumptions
by observing prototype use

Chapter 4

Before the Design Sprint: Make a Plan

If you've arrived to this point, you've decided that a design sprint is applicable to your idea or project and you need to know where to start. In this chapter, we'll show you what you'll need to do to get ready for your design sprint, from defining the scope, to crafting agendas, selecting participants, and even to setting up your own "sprint kit." By the end of this chapter, you will have primed the pump and be ready to turn on the spigot.

Determine the Timebox

D esign sprints work best as a one-week exercise, Monday through Friday, where each phase takes one day. This timebox allows time for enough depth, while the constraints lead to accelerated results. This one-week schedule is the most common practice and recommended as a priority for your team.

Sometimes this schedule just isn't possible, or the needs are a bit different. As mentioned in Chapter 3, there are a number of alternative approaches to a design sprint; whatever your time availability is, your preparation is as important as the work you'll do before and after the design sprint itself. All the participants should be sent the agenda beforehand and see examples of what the results of a design sprint might look like; however, we discourage an over-engineered approach to the expected result. For example, it's not useful to enter a design sprint with an exhaustive feature list because it could prejudice the outcome of the sprint, which may be something very different altogether. If you're reading this book, we assume you're on the right track!

Construct the Agenda/s

Each phase has associated objectives and should have an agenda. We provide a recommended agenda in each chapter for the phases. The days should be short—seven hours is ideal. The days are intense and can be tiring, so plan plenty of breaks. A good rule of thumb is to take a break every 80 to 120 minutes.

With that schedule, there's room for exercises to go over time when needed, and attendees can have set time slots to be available to answer urgent issues.

A "plan-to-be-flexible" approach is best. The agenda should have a prescribed list of exercises and associated timeboxes. The nonnegotiable part of the approach should remain the design sprint steps. The specifics of the timing and exercises used during these steps can be adjusted to fit your project's constraints. Overall, we have noticed that the discipline of the timeboxing is essential to structuring the work. In situations where you don't have timeboxing, you run the risk of participants running over time on one exercise, leaving no time for subsequent exercises.

When crafting your agenda, you might consider a backup if you're first starting out, as you do not yet have experience to guide you when things take a left turn. When Kayla Doan, an Innovation Catalyst at the Constant Contact InnoLoft, finished her design sprint training and was tasked with running them on her own, she created a plan for each sprint she was to facilitate. Then she made a backup of a project that had a different time constraint and used different exercises. But she wasn't done there—she made yet another backup of a scenario that used different problem statements and exercises: "I'd look to see how I think the design sprint would go and then create a plan B and plan C. This helped in those moments when I needed to change gears—I didn't need to resort to calling a break or some other intervention. Always have a contingency plan." A plan B and plan C usually include backup exercises planned at various stages. Make sure to include a few optional exercises that you can turn to at different points of the sprint. If it all blows up, take a break. Then go back to the drawing board. Literally.

Set the Scope

What are the guardrails of the sprint? Scoping a design sprint often includes interviewing stakeholders and doing some research. Determining who in your organization may have input to this project can be a challenge if you work in an organization that has thousands of employees. Short 20-minute interviews ahead of the sprint with the right people can help you determine not only the scope, but also who should be in the room.

The size of the scope depends on a number of variables. What stage is the product in: Early stage? Pre-Market? New-to-market? Mature? A scope that is too broad will be too difficult to wrangle, and a scope that is too narrowly defined will not have enough meat for a full sprint. An example of a scope that is too broad: We want to rethink digital marketing. Too narrow: We want to fix the login page. Just right: We want to explore new ways to engage our users in a brand ambassador program.

A well-scoped design sprint needs to be flexible, especially if it's quickly discovered that the greatest user or business need is outside that scope. However, this scope will be focused on the problem statement described in the Understand phase and used throughout the rest of the sprint. Do not come into the sprint with a challenge statement 100% formed; it's best to have a direction to refine during the Understand phase and honed in the Diverge and Converge phases. We want to exit the sprint with something that will have the greatest impact on the business and our users.

Pick a Facilitator

It helps if you have the luxury of bringing in an external facilitator to run the sprint with you. A web search will reveal dozens of design-thinking experts that might be able to help with this; however, not all will truly see the application of design sprints, as they are a combination of Agile and design thinking. When C. Todd ran the first design sprint at Constant Contact, he hired a consultant from DesignIt, a global design agency, to facilitate. It was a huge help not only to have an objective third party present, but also to have someone in the room with knowledge of the design-thinking framework.

Rie Yamaoka, a UX Manager of Consumer Products at Trulia, hired Dana Mitroff-Silvers for one of the company's first design sprints based on past workshops where she facilitated and was left exhausted. Being both facilitator and participant can be daunting: "I was like, 'I want somebody to just run this whole thing. Tell us how it's done,' instead of me trying to figure out what to do and read about it and read about it and then try to put it in practice while designing at the same time."

Having an external facilitator is desirable but rarely happens in practice. What's most common is to ask one of the selected participants to facilitate the sprint. The appointed facilitator will also be speaking often and leading the group, so they'll need to let everyone have their say and not just push their own agenda. At first blush, many believe the product owner or product manager should lead the sprint, but we caution against that, because the owners/managers will have the most attachment to the outcome. Whoever has the most exposure to design sprints and good facilitation skills would be the best choice, and that might just be you. Don't worry—if you're reading this book, we've got your back, and you're on the right track. In many cases, there is no facilitator, so it may be up to you—yes, you!—to lead the sprint. We cannot say it enough: *it's important to truly facilitate and not to use the facilitator position to push any agenda*. Your goal is to move things forward and ensure everyone can speak at the right times.

What Makes a Good Facilitator?

The ability to listen, adapt, and remain as objective as possible during the sprint. Everyone has a bias, and as mindful as you can be of that bias, there must be an effort to remain neutral throughout the sprint. This will be important in allowing those who have ideas that may seem wild at first to continue to drive to the crazy idea. After all, the crazy idea of strangers sleeping in your house turned into a billion-dollar business (i.e., Airbnb).

The facilitator's role is to monitor progress continually and keep the time. If an exercise is slotted for three minutes, it's the facilitator's job to enforce that. As we've mentioned already, the timeboxed nature of a design sprint might produce some anxiety, but it will force you to produce results. Some teams have shared the time-keeper responsibility rather than have the facilitator enforce it throughout. This can promote a sense of togetherness in the timeboxing.

Facilitators wield the power of the pen, and one tactic is to allow all participants to hold such power. When you write down what others say, be sure to write as close to what they say as possible. In fact, if you can write exactly what they say, it's all the better. Why? Because you show the team members that their input is valuable, and seeing it written exactly as it was said is gratifying to the individual. It's subconscious, but others will notice, and it helps to set the right tone for the design sprint. If a participant says something completely off base, then you can use your facilitator skills to say "so what I'm hearing from you is…" and then write a more appropriate version.

Recruit and Inform Team Members

We recommend a one-page "Here's what you can expect" session plan that informs all participants of the basic questions: What's the objective? Where is it held? Who will be there? What time(s)? What's the outcome?

The ideal team for your design sprint will be about four or five people. Fewer than this, and you're going to struggle to finish all the work ahead. More than this, and you'll start to have some friction around "who does what" and making sure everyone is included. In the spirit of writing this book for the real world, we know four to five people might not be possible. Certainly we have seen groups as small as two and groups with dozens of participants. Be advised that the size of the group can affect the outcome. Too big and you can have an unwieldy number of ideas and the Converge phase will be a challenge; too little and you risk not having enough different viewpoints in the room.

Often, it's wise to include those who have been through the design sprint process before. Jürgen Spangl, Head of Design at Atlassian, cautioned, "If you tried to do it with too many people at the same time who didn't have this experience, it was usually too much explanation, constantly restating why we are doing it." By having others in the room who have been through this before, you can better proceed without too much start-and-stop for educational purposes. This is why Dana Mitroff-Silvers runs an educational exercise at the start of a design sprint where no one has any prior design sprint experience (more on that in Chapter 5).

One important note regarding participants: if there's a person who can veto the results, having that person present for as long as possible during the sprint is advisable. If they are unable to attend, there's a possibility that any progress will come to a screeching halt. You've heard of the HiPPO stampede?[1] Do whatever you can to prevent that from happening. To make the team selection task a little easier, we've created three separate lists; one for startups, one for bigger companies, and one for design firms (or consultants).

A small organization, such as a startup

The participants in a small organization will include the following:

- **Product Manager** It's probably you. If it's not you, you'll want to find the person who has the highest responsibility for getting the product built.

- **Designer** Specifically, a digital product designer or UI designer. An illustrator or graphic designer without web/digital experience is not going to be able to translate ideas into designs efficiently.

- **Engineer or Developer** This person will be a core team member responsible for leading development of the project. If you're a small startup, this might be your technical cofounder or CTO. Again, a little frontend experience goes a long way. If you're asking questions that impact device functionality, you'll be glad you included someone with experience dealing with accessibility, load times, and transitions.

- **Customer-Facing Expert** In a small startup, almost everyone will have some contact with customers. Your designers and developers and founding team will all have frequent contact with the customers. If they don't, you have bigger issues. However, if there's a single person responsible for customer support, that person will definitely need to be included.

---

1 A "HiPPO" refers to the "Highest Paid Person's Opinion," and it can ruin many good things.

- **CEO or Founder** Including the CEO is tricky, so there are some guidelines you can follow to get it right. In smaller companies and startups, it's inevitable and important that the CEO is present. If she is also out trying to close deals or raise money, then at the very least have her be there at the start of the sprint and at the end. Design sprints should never be used to get around the task of getting buy-in from the CEO. As Keith Hopper, former Director of Strategy and Product Innovation at NPR, states, "Design sprints shouldn't be a mechanism to bypass the CEO or they'll never work. People will be looking for [the CEO's] blessing and buy-in on everything anyway." The CEO can also be useful as a tiebreaker when you're stuck. The key is not letting the CEO's opinion override customer needs when the two are obviously contradictory.

- **Marketing Manager or CMO** The marketing manager's viewpoints on positioning and marketing messaging are essential to having the right visuals and copy in the prototype. Just don't let that supersede the need to get something built quickly. Nitpicking on copywriting options will jeopardize meeting your deadline.

A team in a larger enterprise organization

The participants in a larger organization will include the following:

- **Chief Product Officer (CPO), Product Manager, Director or Owner** You may not have the CPO, but you'll need a product person there. For complex projects, we sometimes see more than one person in charge of different aspects of the same product. Include them all if you feel they are all going to help you make the sprint a success.

- **Project Manager** In some cases, there might even be a product manager and a project manager overseeing a product design. Again, include them both. If you're wondering what the difference is between a product manager and a project manager, read the sidebar on page 58.

- **Designer** This should be a competent UI designer. If you have a big group and are going to be producing several prototypes, we recommend including another designer.

- **Engineer or Developer** In our experience, this will most likely be a frontend developer but you might have a backend specialist on the team too. Either way, because you're going to be designing the prototype of your product interface, the more frontend experience, the better.

- **Customer-Facing Expert** In larger companies, this is a defined role: "Customer Support Manager" or "Chief Feel-Good Director" or something like that. If you have more than one customer segment, you might want to have an additional person in here from the marketing team.

- **CEO** See earlier explanation on page 55.

- **Product Marketing Manager** The marketing manager's viewpoints on positioning and marketing messaging are essential to having the right visuals and copy in the prototype.

The studio, agency, or consulting model

The participants in this type of organization will include the following:

- **UX Strategist or Product Lead** If you work at a design firm, then this is probably you. If it's not, you'll want the person tasked with leading the project from the agency or consulting side of the fence.

- **UI Designer** If your team has designers experienced i design sprints, deep dives, or any structured design thinking, that will help provide momentum and efficiency.

- **Engineer or Developer** See earlier explanation.

- **Project Manager** For most design firms, this will be a more typical project manager role. In some ways, this person will be one of the most important members of the team. The project manager will capture all the conversations, sketches, and decisions and will help make sure the team stays on schedule and meets deliverable deadlines.

- **The client** Probably a good idea, right?

Third parties, such as partners, vendors, and advisors to the client, also need to be considered. The client might feel compelled to invite these types of people because they fear leaving them out might alienate them. The choices here can be sorted out by applying the Chicken and Pig Test. The story goes that when preparing breakfast, the chicken's contribution means they are simply involved, while the pig is totally committed. Committed people have a lot to lose if things don't go well, while involved people are mostly bystanders. For a design sprint, it's always better to have the people who are committed than those who are just involved. The test is to ask, is this person involved or committed?

We've also seen suggestions to include "anybody else who's interested." This is inadvisable. More is not better: design sprints are not for anyone. They work best when you include the product team and the people who directly influence the product's success. Including the office manager because he says he once spoke to a customer is just a waste of everyone's time.

What Is the Difference Between Product Management and Project Management?

There's an ongoing confusion as to the difference between product management and project management. Let's try clear this up once and for all. Product managers are responsible for the overall product vision, directing the people (including all the touchy-feely stuff) and the road map (the strategy) for getting there. Project managers are responsible for getting the logistics, scheduling, planning, and task allocations done. Think of the product manager as the CEO of the product and the project manager as its COO. Another way to think about is that the product manager is in charge of the *why* while the project manager is in charge of the *how*.

Regardless of the company size or structure, these roles need to be distinct. In a service company like a design consultancy, the product manager is normally a member of the client team and the project manager is normally a person on the design service team. At Fresh Tilled Soil, the company insists on having a project manager on every project. If the client offers to provide a project manager, Fresh Tilled Soil will still provide its own project manager to ensure that the team has all the support it needs to be awesome. Responsibilities such as updating schedules, managing task lists, coordinating phone calls and meetings, and staying on track with sprint schedules should not be passed off on designers and developers when they have so much else to do.

Secure and Prepare the Space

The physical space in which you host a design sprint is crucial. Secure this space for the duration of the design sprint. It's inadvisable to move to a new space each day, as this will disrupt the work and create gaps in workflow when whiteboards are erased or Post-it notes get lost between sessions. We recommend having a room that contains ample wall space and whiteboards, with room to move about. For tables and chairs for larger sprints, we usually configure the room into "pods" with four to six people at each pod. The Fresh Tilled Soil team has five dedicated spaces with large walls painted with IdeaPaint. This allows us to commit a team to a room for the duration of a design sprint.

It's recommended that participants attend in person; however, design sprints can still work if people are in different cities and can't afford to travel. If the days are consecutive, you want the same room for each remote group so everything stays in place between days. Ensure a solid remote setup and that the remote party can upload its materials immediately as they're created. Let's be very clear here—remote design sprints are not easy. You will need an experienced facilitator. You will also need to plan around time zone differences and schedules and allow for additional time for technical issues, which inevitably come up.

For example, at thoughtbot, a client wanted a design sprint in NYC but had one participant who needed to participate remotely from Portland, OR. We double-checked everyone's connectivity and communication tools before we started, and created a Trello board where everyone uploaded their sketches, storyboards, wireframes, and other content as soon as it was created.

Stock Up on Supplies

Yes, we love Post-it notes and Sharpies, whiteboards, and good old-fashioned paper. Here's what's in our "sprint kit:"

- **Post-it notes** A variety of colors, avoiding darker colors like purple and blue, as black Sharpies tend not to show up well on them, especially in photos. Get two sizes at a minimum: 3 × 3 and 5 × 7. Super-sticky preferable. (And yes, we think 3M should sponsor this book. Are you reading this 3M marketers?)
- **Drawing markers** Any standard black or blue pen is probably fine.
- **Whiteboard markers** Black and red are great.
- **Whiteboards** Self-explanatory. Not much good without markers though.
- **Dot stickers** For voting. You want something small with a few colors. Red/yellow/green are recommended.
- **8.5 × 11 or A4 blank copy paper** Preferably thicker than typical copy paper. We found that copy paper tends to bleed and can leave marks on tables.
- **Snacks** Sugar and carbs are your friends.
- **Coffee** Seriously, caffeine is your friend.
- **Adhesive putty** To stick things to the walls or windows.
- **Easel pads** To put up on the walls, so that they stay nice (alternatively, you can use IdeaPaint everywhere, like Richard does).

It's also nice to have the following items:
- Large ½-inch thick **foam core boards** sized 4' × 6' or larger.
- **Camera** Your mobile phone works quite well (unless you have an old Nokia flip phone).
- **Timer** Optional, though totally awesome. Your mobile phone can work as a substitute, but nothing motivates people like a big clock timer.

What's in Your Sprint Kit?

By Ethan Bagley

Preparation for design sprints happens long before the wrapping comes off the Post-it notes. Make sure each sprint is the best it can be. Assemble your supplies methodically, because every sprint is a little bit different. Discuss what might be needed with the sponsor ahead of time. Keep in mind the space the sprint will take place in, the participants, and any activity-specific needs.

Some things are obvious: Post-it notes, pens and markers, printer paper. As sprint planning continues, other things will become obvious, too: will there be any projection? (Bring the right cables and adapters!) Are any of the activities timeboxed? (Bring a timer!) Are you using whiteboards? (Bring dry-erase markers and erasers!) Most supplies are inexpensive, and will show their value when they're suddenly (sometimes unexpectedly) necessary.

Of course, not everything about a sprint kit needs to be functional. It's important for participants (and facilitators) to have fun, too. Include supplies for a funky warm-up exercise. Bring a wireless speaker for some up-tempo beats while participants are working. Keep participants happy (and healthy) with drinks and snacks for energy throughout the sprint.

Be ready. Build a kit that works for any situation, or be strategic and build a sprint-specific kit. Ensure the tools necessary for a successful sprint are ready when the participants are.

Barnes & Noble Booksellers #2274
313 Corte Madera Town Center
Corte Madera, CA 94925
415-927-9016

STR:2274 REG:004 TRN:5775 CSHR:Nigel F

Design Sprint: A Practical Guidebook for
    9781491923177   T1
    (1 @ 34.99)   34.99

Subtotal   34.99
Sales Tax T1 (9.000%)   3.15
TOTAL   38.14
VISA DEBIT   38.14
    Card#: XXXXXXXXXXXX9496

A MEMBER WOULD HAVE SAVED   3.50

Thanks for shopping at
Barnes & Noble

101.37A   03/17/2016 12:04PM

CUSTOMER COPY

Return Policy

With a sales receipt or Barnes & Noble.com packing slip, a full refund in the original form of payment will be issued from any Barnes & Noble Booksellers store for returns of undamaged NOOKs, new and unread books, and unopened and undamaged music CDs, DVDs, vinyl records, toys/games and audio books made within 14 days of purchase from a Barnes & Noble Booksellers store or Barnes & Noble.com with the below exceptions:

A store credit for the purchase price will be issued (i) for purchases made by check less than 7 days prior to the date of return, (ii) when a gift receipt is presented within 60 days of purchase, (iii) for textbooks, (iv) when the original tender is PayPal, or (v) for products purchased at Barnes & Noble College bookstores that are listed for sale in the Barnes & Noble Booksellers inventory management system.

Opened music CDs, DVDs, vinyl records, audio books may not be returned, and can be exchanged only for the same title and only if defective. NOOKs purchased from other retailers or sellers are returnable only to the retailer or seller from which they are purchased, pursuant to such retailer's or seller's return policy. Magazines, newspapers, eBooks, digital downloads, and used books are not returnable or exchangeable. Defective NOOKs may be exchanged at the store in accordance with the applicable warranty.

Returns or exchanges will not be permitted (i) after 14 days or without receipt or (ii) for product not carried by Barnes & Noble or Barnes & Noble.com.

Return Policy

With a sales receipt or Barnes & Noble.com packing slip, a full refund in the original form of payment will be issued from any Barnes & Noble Booksellers store for returns of

Ethan's sprint kit:

- Very small Post-its (assorted colors, 2" × 1.5", 200–300)
- Small, square Post-its (assorted colors, 3"× 3", 1,000–1,500)
- Small, square Post-its (yellow, 3"× 3", 1,000–1,500)
- Medium, long Post-its (assorted colors, 4"× 6", 50–100)
- Medium, long Post-its (assorted colors, 6"× 8", 50–100)
- Sharpies (black, 12)
- Sharpies (assorted colors, 12)
- Pens (black, 12)
- Pens (blue, 12)
- Dry-erase markers (black, 12)
- Dry-erase markers (assorted colors, 4–6 per color)
- 8.5"× 11" plain printer paper (heavy weight: 35+lbs., 50 sheets)
- Index cards (unlined, 200)
- Pushpins (100)

- Dot stickers (assorted colors, 200)
- Painter's tape (1" roll)
- Name tents (12)
- EXPO White Board Care Cleaning Spray (Dry-erase cleaning fluid, 1 bottle)
- Dry-erase cleaning eraser (1–2)
- Display adapters (VGA, DVI, HDMI - PC, Mac)
- HDMI - Thunderbolt
- VGA - Thunderbolt
- DVI - Thunderbolt
- HDMI - VGA
- DVI - VGA
- DVI - HDMI
- Display cables (HDMI, VGA)
- HDMI
- VGA
- Audio cables (3.5mm stereo audio cable)
- Time Timer (7")
- Speaker (small, Bluetooth and 3.5" inputs)

Conduct a Pre-Mortem

To prepare for and prevent the things that can go wrong (and ask any of us, many things can!) we recommend conducting a "pre-mortem" before the design sprint begins. It's like a port-mortem, though you're predicting why the project will fail before even producing it. Stacey Dyer of iZotope uses these religiously: "Instead of asking what could go wrong with that feature, imagine it has completely flopped and has now become an epic fail."

It's a simple exercise you can do with the project sponsor: first, imagine that the design sprint has miserably failed. Second, consider the plausible reasons for this design sprint's failure. Then review these fail-points and discover ways to strengthen the project.

Let's now take a look at some standard things that can go wrong, and what you can do to fix them.

What happened?	The fix!
Room was too warm. People fell asleep.	Make sure room is at a comfortable temperature.
The team was hungry.	Buy cookies. We prefer chocolate chip.
Everyone was on their computers all the time.	Establish a "no devices" rule except when reviewing existing materials online. Come prepared with lots of pens and paper and Post-its to write on. Or just conduct the sprint in Tahiti. We hear there's no signal there.
The main stakeholder ducked out for meetings when key decisions were made, then came back and reversed them.	Ensure the key stakeholder has the time reserved on her calendar.
An executive came in mid-sprint and derailed the team.	Involve the executive earlier in the design sprint, or at least get them to help set the course/tone.
People ran out of steam.	Take frequent breaks. We recommend a short break every 80 to 120 minutes as a humane duration for focused work.
Exercises went way over time.	Set timeboxes for exercises and use timers!

Prepare and Distribute Background Materials

Before the sprint, request that each participant send background material that you can organize for the team to review. These can include, but are not limited to:

- A list of apps, sites, or products similar to parts of what you want to create, as well as others with aspects you may wish to emulate.

- Any existing materials you already have on hand, such as pitch decks, user stories, wireframes, or prototypes. These are great background materials, but don't flesh these out more than you already have. The design sprint will move these forward, and what you come to at the end of the sprint will likely be different.

- Information about each of your key customer types: who they are, their stories, and how they feel about the problem you're working to solve. If there's documentation from interviews you conducted with them, that's great to have too. Of all the things to do pre-design sprint, this requires the most lead time, so you'll want to start identifying and scheduling users first.

Schedule Time with Users

For the Test phase of the sprint, you'll need to schedule time with users. Sometimes you'll need to schedule a few interviews on the first day as well (foreshadowing: Discovery Interviews, more in Chapter 5). Bookending a design sprint with customers can be very powerful. Should you choose to conduct Discovery Interviews in the first phase, you don't want those same users on test day. One or two is fine, but not all. Scheduling these appointments before the sprint begins will save you from scrambling as you have a deadline to get everything ready for testing on the final day. The downside is you may not be able to schedule with the "right" users until the end of the first day, as you'll define who these users are during that phase. If the desired user type drifts from who is intended, you may need to cancel some sessions and reschedule with users who are better matches to the type you seek.

Based on Steve Krug's guidance in *Rocket Surgery Made Easy: The Do-It-Yourself Guide to Finding and Fixing Usability Problems*, we recommend six to seven users for 30–60 minutes as ideal, though if users are very hard to come by, schedule longer sessions for fewer users. For example, we recently did a design sprint where the target user was the manager of a factory floor. These people were hard to come by, so we spoke with two users for 90 minutes each instead of six users for 30 minutes each. This approach gave us a lot of great information, but there's always a caution that you're designing a product for a small market, so be sure to consider the outcomes of these interviews and take into consideration the quantity versus quality debate. You'll need to finish by late afternoon to prepare findings for an end-of-day discussion that will conclude the design sprint. Each participant will use the prototype and be asked questions to get their feedback.

Post-it Note Pro Tip

Many people peel a Post-it straight up and off, but the problem with that is the edge where there is adhesive curls. Even if you flatten this when sticking to a vertical surface, the Post-it does not lay flat. The best way to peel the Post-it off is to pull it from the side as flat as possible. The result is that the Post-it will lay flat on the surface, and also there's less chance of it falling off.

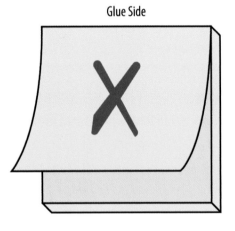

Glue Side

DON'T: Peel post-its from bottom to top.
They will bend and not lie flat.

Glue Side

DO: Peel post-its from the side.

Takeaways:

- Agree and align on the scope (not too narrow, not too broad).

- Select a facilitator and recruit your team to have the right mix of different viewpoints in the sprint.

- Set the daily agendas and circulate to the team so they have an idea of what to expect.

- Get your space and supplies ready.

- Co-create guidelines and rules of engagement at the start.

- Prepare background materials.

- Schedule time with users in advance, if possible.

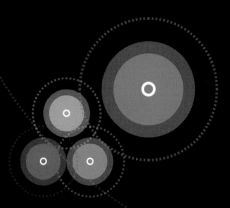

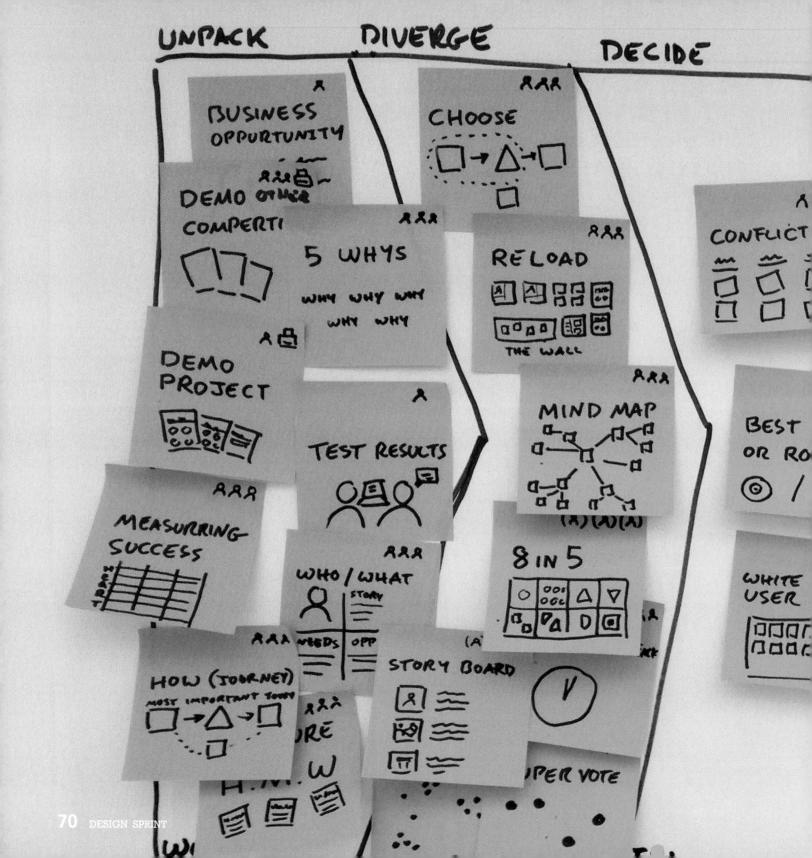

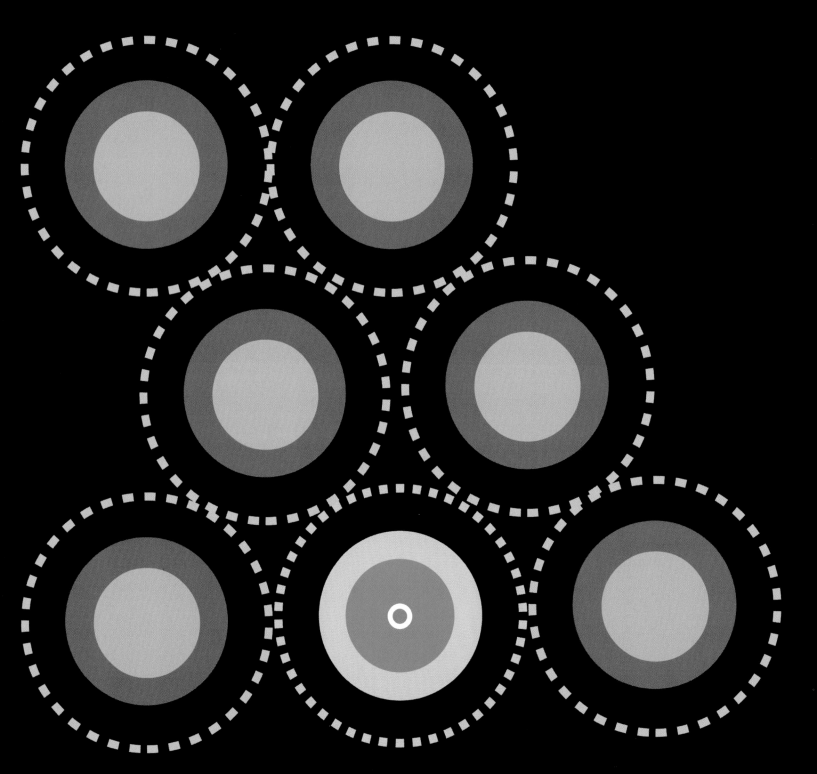

Chapter 5

Phase 1: Understand

The first day of a design sprint is primarily an opportunity to bring the working team to a mutual understanding of the problem to be solved. If the team members haven't already met one another, then this is the time when everyone will get acquainted. Getting to know each other helps to develop empathy, which is a cornerstone of any design-thinking exercise. In this chapter, we'll give you tools and exercises to help break the ice and inject a little fun into the process. These exercises will also help you get inspired. Whether you need to be inspired by facts or out-of-the-box ideas, we've included a collection of tools to get you there. Together you'll answer the questions: "Who is the customer, who is the user, and what are their problems?" You'll all share the relevant context so the answers to these questions can be understood clearly, but you won't need to come up with solutions yet.

What Happens During the Understand Phase?

Get the Background	~1.5 hours
Get Inspired	~1.5 hour
Define the Problem	~1 hour
Know the User	~3 hours

As discussed in Chapter 4, a design sprint is a flexible framework, and you'll need to adapt it to your particular situation. If the conversation requires it, exercises can be added, reordered, skipped, shortened, or extended. Your mileage may vary on the duration for each of the exercises; we've done journey maps in 15 minutes, and some have taken up to three hours. It all depends on the level of detail your project needs.

Whatever you do, don't forget to take frequent breaks and get a good lunch! (Yum.)

You might not finish these exercises by the end of the first day. In that case, do the retrospective at the end of the day, then continue the exercises on the second day. If that happens, be sensitive to the time constraints to finish up the background work so that you have enough time for the additional phases of the design sprint.

Recommended Agenda

Get the Background

Introductions	~15 minutes
Introduce the Idea Parking Lot	~ 5 minutes
Review Agenda	~ 5 minutes
Rules of the Design Sprint	~ 5 minutes
Pitch Practice #1	~10 minutes
Review Research and Past Work	~60 minutes

Get Inspired

Goals and Anti-Goals	~30 minutes
Existing Product, Competitors, and Substitutes	~40 minutes
Facts and Assumptions	~20 minutes
Question Formulation Technique	~15 minutes (optional)

Define the Problem

Problem Statement	~30 minutes
Reframe the Problem with Challenge Maps	~30 minutes (optional)

Know the User

Who-Do	~10 minutes
Personas	~45 minutes
Customer Interviews	~60 minutes
User Journey Map	~60 minutes

Wrap-up

Daily Retrospective	~15 minutes
Team Drinks	~60 to 90 minutes (optional)

Get the Background

The goal for this part of the day is to understand all the relevant data and information on hand. The team should explore what they know and what they don't know to gauge what knowledge gaps exist for the problem. You'll cover existing research done before the design sprint and review analysis of competitive or similar product offerings.

Introductions

Give the design sprint team the opportunity to introduce themselves. Everyone should say their name and their role in the design sprint team and the project to follow. The facilitator can go first to set the stage and provide a good example, followed by the main product sponsor or stakeholder, followed by the rest of the team going around in a circle.

Depending on how familiar the team members are with each other you could include an icebreaker to get the team to open up and be comfortable working together. You'll be spending an intense few days together—might as well get the edge off up front!

How

1. Select your icebreaker from the list on the next page or another you know how to do already.
2. Describe your icebreaker to the group.
3. Blueprint it by going first to set the stage and give an example for everyone.
4. Pick an order and go around the room and make sure that each person completes the icebreaker.

Difficulty: Easy

Size: The whole group

Materials: 5 × 7 index cards to fold

Don't let someone talk for a long time. This is a time for simple introductions, not for people to drone on about their background and opinions

Approximate time: 30 to 60 seconds per participant

A Few of Our Favorite Icebreakers

Word Ball: Bring a plush ball. Toss the ball to someone else in the room, and as you throw it, say a random word. Each person does the same thing in turn, until everyone's had a chance to throw the ball.

What Neighborhood Do You Live In?: Great for people in cities who love to talk about their 'hoods. At the end of each person's intro, each person says the neighborhood they live in. One of Trace's favorites.

Draw Your Name and Draw _____: Give each participant an index card and ask them to fold them in half: on one side, they should write their names in a decorative font, and something tangential and/or related to the topic of the week. For example, at a recent sprint, C. Todd asked everyone present to draw how they'd make pancakes. The manager present drew a car and an International House of Pancakes sign (he liked their blueberry syrup).

Little-Known Fact: Ask participants to state their name, title, and/or function, then add a fact that no one in the room likely knows about them.

Hopes and Fears: We learned about this one from Karen Cross at Atlassian. She uses this to help bring out potential project issues, in addition to getting others to know one another:

"It's basically a 20-minute brainstorm exercise at the very beginning of a sprint. Everyone sits, and has two colored Post-its (usually red and blue). Depending on the number of people involved, I usually limit them to maybe three hopes and two fears, two hopes, or maybe one hope. And then everyone writes them down, and they all put them face down in the middle of the table, and then they draw from them, and then have to read someone else's and explain what they think it means. By doing that, it gets them to be empathetic [to one another]."

After the introductions, acknowledge the others involved with the project but not participating in the design sprint.

Introduce the Idea Parking Lot

After that, introduce the concept of the Idea Parking Lot. During the sessions, the team may generate ideas or have other "aha" moments that may not apply to the main topic, or they may propose solutions on the first day that shouldn't be explored until the Diverge phase. An Idea Parking Lot is a place where such ideas and topics can be captured, so you can come back to them when you're ready. Unlike a real parking lot (especially during the holidays), there's always room in the Idea Parking Lot!

How

1. Place a large piece of paper on the wall. A page from a Post-it easel pad is ideal.
2. Label it "Idea Parking Lot" at the top. Draw a picture of a car. Drawing pictures of cars is fun.
3. Throughout the sprint, when anyone has an idea you want to capture that doesn't fit the sprint, write it on a small Post-it and stick it in the Idea Parking Lot.

Difficulty: Easy
Size: The whole group
Materials: Post-its (you can also use a Google Doc or Trello Board)
Approximate time: 3–5 minutes

Review Agenda

There's a lot to cover on the first day of the design sprint. Give the team a sense of what's to come, so they know what to expect.

How

1. Review the printed agenda, or bring it up on a large TV screen.
2. In about a sentence each, describe the exercises you'll be doing.

Difficulty: Easy
Size: The whole group
Materials: A printed agenda (or a large TV screen)

Don't go into too much detail.

Approximate time: 5 minutes

Rules of the Design Sprint

It might seem strange to start a creative thinking process by establishing rules. This counterintuitive approach is often shunned by the uninitiated as being restrictive or dampening the creative process. This couldn't be further from the truth.

The guidelines we recommend are intended to level the playing field for all participants. Human beings are complicated enough without the additional pressure of having to solve problems while stuck in a room full of peers or strangers for five days, some of whom speak more forcefully than others. Put them all in a small space together to understand a problem, generate solutions, and make prototypes, and it can get downright chaotic. The humans involved in the design sprint phases are more than just sources for ideas and hands to make things. They bring with them their own experiences, biases, emotions, preferences, and politics. Guidelines reduce the risk of those biases and focus the team on the customer's problems. Our goal with these guidelines is to get the team to fall in love with solving the problem and not with one of their own subjective solutions.

By providing guidelines and rules for the team, you can empower the team. Again, constraints increase creativity, and these guidelines can help. You reduce the opportunity for mental fatigue and ensure that each person's contributions will be given attention and value.

One of the most important elements of a design sprint is that these are established on day 1 or even before the design sprint begins. These are not guidelines to impose on everyone in an authoritarian fashion—rather, ask the entire team to co-create them. Our recommendation is to select a few from this list (or your own!) then place blank bullet points and ask the team to help you fill them in. If no one adds any to the list, add some yourself. By adding it on the fly, you're more likely to get things moving.

Here's a sampling of guidelines we use. What could you add to this list?

- Everyone participates
- Have one conversation at a time
- Withhold judgment of others' ideas
- Get up and draw
- Be comfortable
- Be easy on people, tough on ideas
- Be timely
- Be present
- The phone stack
- One computer at a time
- No jargon/TPS reports
- No HiPPOS
- No "Yes, but…"

Everyone participates. We mean everyone. Design sprints are not for the faint of heart, nor the introvert that struggles to speak up. Rather, design sprints are intended to encourage participation by all, regardless of roles with the company or project team. There will be mechanisms to allow the quiet voices in the room to be heard, and the facilitator's role (see Chapter 4) is important in identifying who isn't participating and draw them out.

Have one conversation at a time. Have you ever been in a meeting and seen lots of side conversations? We don't want those in a design sprint because we believe that all comments are valuable and want everyone to hear them. This will prevent everyone from talking over one another and prevent she/he-who-speaks-loudest-wins.

Withhold judgment of others' ideas. This is increasingly important during the Diverge phase when participants are generating ideas. To bring forth an idea can be a courageous act, and if there is harsh judgment, it can begin to erode confidence and diminish the quality of ideas. There will be mechanisms for judging ideas and bringing the better ones forward; those are when judgment is necessary and even welcome. So hold judgment until that time arrives.

Be comfortable. We don't want people to feel like they have to stand up or sit down all day, so if someone is sitting and feels the need to stand, or, if they need to leave to go to the restroom, that's OK. It seems almost too obvious to call out, but it does make a difference and establishes the tone of the sprint. Take frequent breaks so everyone stays refreshed and brings their A-game.

Be easy on people, tough on ideas. Along the same lines as withholding judgment, we want people to feel like they can contribute. There's no better way to do that than to value what they contribute and go easy on them for doing so.

Be timely. Timeboxing helps force movement. Facilitators take note: this one is mostly on you. Your job is to make sure the time doesn't go over what was stated and agreed on. If you said you'd have lunch at 12:30 p.m., make sure you're breaking at 12:30 p.m. Otherwise, everyone will be looking at their watches thinking "Weren't we supposed to break for lunch now?" and they will become disengaged. And hangry.

Be present. A design sprint is an intense exercise and many participants will get tired and distracted. Stay in the room, listen intently, and participate actively in the conversations.

The phone stack. Who loves their mobile phones? Most people. Who also doesn't put them down in meetings? Most people. To keep the team focused and avoid the inevitable buzzing phone distraction, we ask everyone to pile their phones up on top of each other. This is known as the phone stack. The first person to reach for the phone might receive a small punishment, such as having to buy the next round of coffees or drinks.

One computer at a time. Sometimes you'll need a computer projecting on a screen to review the agenda, instructions, or materials, but everyone else should keep their computers away. Only one computer should be in use at a time. Unless necessary, refrain from using your computer during the sprint. People will use the computers to multitask and will stop paying attention to the conversation. To take notes, write them down on paper instead. Everyone will be able to listen better when they're looking at one another instead of their screens.

No jargon/TPS reports. Do you know what a TPS report is? Neither do we! Keep the jargon and acronyms to a minimum so everyone in the room understands. If necessary, start an acronym dictionary in the back of the room to keep track and let everyone know what "BTKO" really means.

No HiPPOs. The Highest Paid Person's Opinion can often trample on other people's ideas. Make this a rule so that a senior member doesn't keep junior participants from defending their own points of view.

No "Yes, but…" Any time the word "but" is said, it often invalidates what was said earlier, so "yes, but…" is really a disagreement. Disagreeing is OK, but preceding that disagreement with a "yes" can be subtly counterproductive. There will be times for debate and disagreement in design sprints. Or instead of disagreeing, build on the last idea by saying "Yes, and…" or "Yes, because…"

If you ever see anyone breaking these guidelines during the sprint, call them out on it. If you violate these guidelines, call yourself out. If you are called out, admit it and move on.

After reviewing the rules you'll be following over the next few days, it's time to get started! Proceed with the following exercises to begin the design sprint itself.

Pitch Practice #1

The project sponsor should begin each day by walking the design sprint team through the business opportunity and market, and the problem you're solving as they see it.

Pitch practice makes sure that everyone is aware of the original intent of the sprint, and allows the project sponsor to practice and refine the application's elevator pitch over the week. The pitch can be modified as needed as new information, options, and decisions come to light.

How

1. Have the project sponsor give her elevator pitch. Use a pitch deck if one is available. Cap it to a few minutes.

2. Ensure that she covers the business opportunity, market, and the problem the team wants to solve.

3. Allow quick questions at the end, but save most of the discussion for the rest of the day's activities.

Difficulty: Easy

Size: The whole group

Materials: The project sponsor's brain and her pitch deck if one is available

Don't let the project sponsor drone on and on and on (there's a 12-step program for that called On-and-On-Anon). Keep them timeboxed!

Approximate time: 5–10 minutes

Credit: Alex Baldwin at thoughtbot, Jared Spool for the On-and-On-Anon joke

Review Research and Past Work

Following the pitch, share a deeper dive into the background and motivation for the project. Reviewing the current body of knowledge together will help to get everyone on the same page, and allow people to build upon what has come before.

How

1. Make it clear that what was done previously will inform the activities during the design sprint, but there will be an opportunity to take things in a different direction if it's better.
2. Have a brief discussion of the background information or research that was sent out before the sprint.
3. Go over any other materials or things people know about the problem space but haven't yet shared.
4. Review any previous initiatives, including applications or prototypes the company has made to solve a similar problem.

Difficulty: Easy

Size: The whole group

Materials: Presentations of past project work (if applicable); screenshots or walkthrough of product (if existing); any relevant metrics, perhaps from a business intelligence report or marketing report

Don't overload the team with information. Cognitive (over)load is a thing. Also don't judge or get into debates. There will be plenty of opportunity to discuss different perspectives later in the day and throughout the design sprint.

Approximate time: Up to 1 hour

Credit: The team at thoughtbot

With the guidelines established and the background material covered for this sprint, the team can seek ways of inspiration to create a fantastic product.

Get Inspired

When considering new possibilities, you will want to know where you're starting from so you can later diverge in order to generate a multitude of options. Going into a project, it's important to understand what constitutes success. Everyone on the team arrived with their own notions of what success is. Like the North Star for ships sailing in the 1700s, understanding in detail what the goals are can help you as you search for inspiration and direction.

Goals and Anti-Goals

In this exercise, you'll define the objectives of the project so all get on board and agree with it. This can also help define the project's guardrails.

How

1. Draw two columns on a whiteboard, one for the project's goals, and one for its anti-goals. Anti-goals are things that are explicitly not goals of the project.

2. Ask the team to brainstorm goals for the project. These should be high-level objectives, not features. For example, "Save $75 million per year in increased production efficiency" is a high-level objective, but "Allow users to propose savings ideas" is a feature.

3. As each goal is suggested, allow the team to discuss it and agree that it's a goal for the design sprint or following project. If it's not, move it to the anti-goals column.

4. Ask the team to similarly brainstorm the anti-goals that are not needed for the project's success.

5. Identify the top three goals. Underline the #1 goal.

6. Capture and upload the list so the team can refer to it later.

Difficulty: Easy

Size: The whole group

Materials: Whiteboard and markers

Don't list features, list too many goals. You'll go nuts trying to meet them all.

Approximate time: 30 minutes

Credit: Graham Siener, Pivotal Labs[1]

---

1 *http://bit.ly/pivotal-pov*

Goals

all media types in
One place

all languages- unicode
                support.
RTL language support

- Single Sign On
- Single Platform
- Simple Display & Visualisation
for Complex MetaData

- Search & Filter Data
- aggerated Content from
internal System.
- be as asynchronous
as the pipeline
- Repeated ease of use

Questions:

- Single Sign on
for which websites?

- Real time
updates?

Anti Goals

- No DIY Visualisations

- No Advanced Visualis

- Not to Reuse Suggested
wireframes- but to use insigh
from them to Create new
Simpler wireframes.

- no User-added Content.

- No Insights

Existing Product, Competitors, and Substitutes

As you continue to look for inspiration, it can come from an analogous solution in another industry. A competitor. An elegant solution to a different product you'd like to emulate in some way. With digital products, many solutions exist, so rather than reinvent the wheel, seek out solutions from other industries that might apply to your problem. They don't have to fit your problem exactly (remember, you're only seeking inspiration at this point). We often take a section of a wall and print out apps, screenshots, drawings, or web pages of things we find inspiring, useful, or maybe even want to replicate (or all this can be viewed online and projected onto a screen).

There's a risk of opening Pandora's box here, in that sometimes a team can get too focused on replicating what already exists, instead of solving what a user or customer really needs. Don't spend too much time on a deep dive of each of these; stick to a broad overview.

How

1. Sync your monitor or phone to a large TV screen. Have someone bring up your existing site or app if one already exists, and walk through it to give the participants context. Discuss what's working well and what's not working well.

2. Invite participants to identify competitive and substitute products. Bring them up on the screen, or put a printout up on the wall. Discuss the strengths and weaknesses of each. Also consider what "non-products" are used. For example, when a customer uses pencil and paper to track event participants.

3. Do the same for aspects of apps or sites from other industries. For example, an onboarding flow or data visualization you might want to replicate.

4. Take notes on the areas that are inspiring. If you've put screenshots up, have everyone stick Post-its or dot stickers next to the areas they like the most.

Difficulty: Easy

Size: The whole group

Materials: Printouts or displayed screens of anything that inspires the team

Context: This is a good generative exercise best completed at the start of the sprint.

Don't go too deep or spend too long.

Approximate time: 30–45 minutes

Credit: The team at thoughtbot

Facts and Assumptions

Another way to find inspiration is to acknowledge the biases we each bring to the table, so everyone's aware of them and can overcome them when they need to. It's human to make assumptions and form biases. Just get over it: we are biased. These biases can influence our decisions, which will affect our ability to solve the right problem. Before we can solve tough problems and open new pathways, we need to escape the confines of our existing biases, break out of our mental habits, and call out the assumptions that we may have. Einstein famously observed that "You can't solve problems at the same level of thinking that created them." Pushing our brains to identify all the assumptions we have about a problem will unlock ways for us to try and solve it; facts and assumptions help to reduce your bias by identifying them.

Let's take a simple example: "I went to the supermarket yesterday and bought an apple because I was hungry." How many assumptions do you think are in that statement? More than you think. First, there's an assumption of causality: that being hungry causes the purchase of an apple. We don't know about you, but we often look in our cupboard or refrigerator first before going to the store for an apple. Second, that the supermarket has apples in it. Yes, in the United States this is common, but depending on time of year and location, it is not always true, and hence an assumption.

These same subltle assumptions and biases can haunt you if not properly identified at the start of a project.

This exercise is used to identify what data is on hand, what is still unknown, and most importantly, what assumptions the team is making. This helps to minimize confirmation bias (it *never* is eliminated) and baseline everyone in the room to understand the context of the problem at hand. This also helps to identify what knowledge gaps exist.

How

1. Allow participants 3–10 minutes to individually document facts and assumptions (one fact/assumption per Post-it). Use one color Post-it for facts and another color for assumptions.

2. Invite each participant to share their assumptions as they post them to a wall or display board.

3. Ask participants to rewrite any successfully challenged facts on the assumption colored Post-its.

4. Document questions that arise during the group discussion process.

5. Ask participants to approach the wall or board of facts and assumptions in pairs to work silently grouping the facts and assumptions by commonality.

6. Partway through the process, replace the categorizers with two new participants, allowing them to undo or redo any work previously done; continue to replace categorizers every few minutes until all Post-its are categorized.

7. Once half the Post-its are categorized, give the categorizers medium-sized Post-its to add category headings.

Difficulty: Hard

Size: Individuals, pairs, and the entire group

Materials: Sharpies, medium-sized Post-its, small Post-its in two colors

Context: This is a good generative exercise completed at the start of the sprint. It must be done before determining insights.

Don't let questionable facts go unchallenged, as they may be assumptions (anyone can challenge a fact or an assumption). Let the group jump to insights without a full exploration of the facts and assumptions.

Example: "9% of current customers use feature X" is a fact; "current customers don't understand how to use feature X" is an assumption.

Approximate time: 20–30 minutes

Credit: InnoLoft team at Constant Contact with inspiration from Craig Launcher of Assumption Storming

Question Formulation Technique (QFT)

In addition to our biases, we likely have questions—lots of questions: Will this work? Is my idea as awesome as I think it is? How are users currently solving this problem? What are the best ways for your organization to solve this? A question-storming approach can be quite helpful in understanding the problem you're trying to solve. Phil McKinney, former Hewlett-Packard CTO, made himself into a question specialist for the corporate world, and argues that crafting good questions is what allows people to make innovative breakthroughs: "The challenge is that, as adults, we lose our curiosity over time. We get into ruts, we become experts in our fields or endeavors." Dan Rothstein, founder of The Right Question Institute, studies the art and science of asking questions.

"Wielded with purpose and care, a question can become a sophisticated and potent tool to expand minds, inspire new ideas, and give us surprising power at moments when we might not believe we have any."

Dan and his cofounder Luz Santana created the Question Formulation Technique, which was initially made for teachers to teach children the skill of asking questions. However, we have found that this also helps teams generate questions about the project and uncover some interesting opportunities.

This exercise is used to bring to the surface the questions each participant has about a particular topic. This can align teams so they all know what questions everyone has on a particular topic.

How

1. Provide a question focus: the area that needs exploration.
2. Inform participants about the QFT guidelines:
   a. Ask as many questions as possible.
   b. Do not stop to answer, judge, or to discuss the questions.
   c. Write down every question exactly as it is stated.
   d. Change any statement into a question.
3. Establish a time limit.
4. Post-up and sort per your preference.

Difficulty: Easy

Size: Individual and group

Materials: Sharpies and Post-it notes

Context

This is a divergent exercise, so it is best used in the beginning of a sprint. It could precede or follow Facts and Assumptions. A good follow-up exercise is to converge onto the important questions to answer by voting.

Don't allow questions to be answered—it can be a rat-hole in the making. Don't let this go un-timeboxed.

Approximate time: 5–15 minutes

Source: The QFT is © The Right Question Institute 2011. Used with permission: *http://rightquestion.org*.

By this point in the day, you know which direction to go—you're feeling inspired and you're ready to dig deeper into the problem. If someone comes to you with a problem, most people start thinking about a solution. Hopefully the questions you've generated are more about the problem and not leading to one solution or another, because as soon as you start thinking of a solution, you risk missing out on possibilities for a deeper understanding of the problem.

Define the Problem

What's the problem you're attempting to solve? This is one of the most important aspects and sadly, it is one that's overlooked frequently by the many teams and clients we have worked with. Since most designers and engineers are trained to design and build things, the propensity to create and deliver often overpowers the desire to understand why they are creating something. You can look at the copious amount of digital products that were created and went nowhere. Let's take a look at a few examples you might have heard of.

Airtime, the face-to-face video chat web application that was launched on June 5, 2012 with quite a splash. Shawn Fanning and Sean Parker (the famous Facebook investor), who created Napster, did a number of talk-show appearances and held a launch party that any record company would envy, well, except for the glitches.[2] The result? $33M of funding with no users after 16 months of operation.[3]

What was the problem they were trying to solve for? Skype, Google Hangouts' and Apple's Facetime already had been in the market to solve these needs and Airtime offered little extra in the way of solving for another need. Had Airtime been more focused on the problem of video chat, it could have worked toward a better solution—instead they kept building and didn't pay attention.

---

2 Erin Griffith, "Big Celebs, Big Ideas: The Double-Edged Sword of a Big Flashy Launch," June 5, 2012. *http://bit.ly/celeb-ideas.*

3 Milo Yiannopoulos, "There Is Literally No One Left on Sean Parker's Airtime," October 28th, 2013, *http://bit.ly/yiannopoulos.*

Facebook Home is (or was) a mobile digital product you might have tried on your Android device. We didn't. Did it even make any sense? It seemed to solve a problem for Facebook, which was keeping their users in their app, but it did not solve any real problem or need for the user. We have seen many companies start design sprints to solve their own problems rather than solve a problem for their users and/or customers.

To understand the problem you're solving for, you need to understand what information you have on hand about the current user behavior. Now that you've dug into the data and information you already have, and explored your facts, assumptions, and questions, you'll consider the problems your users have faced. Are there tangential related problems? Are there seemingly unrelated problems? The objective is to paint as complete a picture as possible to understand the context of the situation.

Problem Statement

You can't define a good solution until you understand the problem you're solving. Defining that together gets the team on the same page and sets it as the North Star for the rest of the design sprint. This keeps ideas focused on the problem at hand, and other great ideas that solve a different problem can get added to the Idea Parking Lot.

How

1. Distribute large 3 × 5 Post-its and ask participants to individually write down potential problems the target user might have (one problem per Post-it). The following questions can serve as prompts:

    a. What is the job-to-be-done?[4]

    b. What is the problem that this product or service will solve?

    c. What is the motivation behind what the user wants or needs?

2. Place the Post-its on a whiteboard, grouping similar ones together, drawing lines between them as needed to indicate themes.

3. Discuss the problem statement, and agree on the general problem to be solved.

4. Refine the problem statement and finalize the wording.

5. Rewrite the problem statement in a large format on a whiteboard or big Post-it and keep it visible throughout the sprint. This will be important to reflect and revisit if the conversation veers too far from the established problem.

Difficulty: Medium

Size: The whole group

Materials: Whiteboard, markers, and large Post-its

Don't write a compound problem statement that solves all problems and tries to be all things to all people. Use conjunctions like "and" and "or" sparingly, if at all. In addition, don't try to solve the problem yet. You're just trying to understand it.

Approximate time: 20 minutes

Credit: The team at thoughtbot

---

4 Clayton Christensen Institute, "Jobs to Be Done," *http://www.christenseninstitute.org/key-concepts/jobs-to-be-done/.*

Students don't Rece[ive]
[e]nough guidance on ho[w]
[to] develop the skills that
[e]nable them to learn
[and] flourish.

Reframe the Problem with Challenge Maps

Now that we've defined the problem, how might we reframe the challenge given what we collectively know? Taking all the information in, you may realize that your initial hypothesis might be the wrong one. If so, that's great! You'll congratulate yourself as this process has worked for you. As we mentioned earlier, there are plenty of stories about products being built that no one needs nor wants.

Why reframe? Often we see organizations thinking and speaking in terms of their features and their products, not the customer or the user's eyes (the paying customer and the user may not be the same person).

For example, have you ever purchased a pair of socks? Our guess is you probably have purchased many socks over your lifetime, and they are always sold in pairs.

In 2003, Jonah Staw, a product designer at the prestigious Frog Design was joking with Arielle Eckstut about how they could solve the problem of missing socks by wearing all the surviving socks that did not match. That silly joke inspired them to start LittleMissMatched. They reframed the problem from "I have missing socks" to "I can combine and wear these leftover socks" to "None of my socks match, and that's awesome!" They sold socks in "pairs" of three that have matching color palettes but no matching design patterns. Your suit-wearing Wall Street businesswoman might not wear them, but 11-year-old girls absolutely loved it. Eleven years later, the company is reportedly grossing over $30M annually in sales.[5]

The ability to reframe a situation can lead to incredible breakthroughs, and it can also lead to small insights that you can leverage to delight your users. It all depends on

---

5 *http://bit.ly/mismatched-socks*

your perspective and the ability to shift perspective once you have all the context in front of your team. If you ask a team of engineers how to improve the experience of the Amtrak ride between Boston and New York City, they may offer all sorts of suggestions for improvements in the rail structures, suspensions on the train, and more comfortable seating. However, for the amount of funding it would take to implement that type of system and infrastructure, you might also be able to hire exceptional waitstaff as servers to serve top-shelf liquor and gourmet hors d'oeuvres to passengers during the trip. Rather than a shorter trip, passengers may start requesting a longer duration.[6]

This reframed the problem from a structural, smooth ride to creating an experience. The effort to improve that experience could be a much smaller implementation. These are the little details you'll want to seek out as you reframe the problem you're solving.

A technique that can help with this is to create challenge maps. A challenge map asks the questions "Why?" and "What's stopping you?" and forces you to consider the relationship between the possibilities. Once you've created a challenge map around a particular issue, you can start to see what might be blocking the way to a solution. Many times you start out in one area and learn that's not the area you need to focus on! With challenge maps, you can explore the problem you've identified and determine whether you need to restate it, reframe it, or solve a different problem altogether.

---

6   From Rory Sutherland's TED talk (*http://bit.ly/brand-over-brain*)

Challenge Maps

How

1. Divide into pairs or small groups.

2. Write the Problem Statement on a large Post-it note, and place it in the center of a whiteboard or a flipchart page. Add "How Might We" (or "HMW" for short) before the text of the Post-it.

3. Challenge this initial statement by asking the group "Why should we do this?"

4. Answer that "why" question on another Post-it note and place it above the initial Post-it note. Add "How Might We" to the beginning of it. Now challenge that new statement with the same "why should we do this?" question, adding Post-its going upward. Repeat this until a natural endpoint is reached (such as "to make more money").

5. You may find there are multiple reasons, so answering "why else?" will lead you to put Post-its to the left or right of each other.

6. In the downward direction, challenge each "How might we…" statement with the question "What's stopping us from doing this?" Answer that question, then rewrite it to a "How might we…" question, and place it below that Post-it.

7. You may also find multiple reasons for what's stopping you. Place Post-it notes to the left or right answering "what else is stopping us?"

8. Continue until a natural endpoint is reached.

9. With the entire group, review the Post-its that were created and see if any of the added statements would make a more applicable Problem Statement. If so, use that Post-it note to revise the Problem Statement accordingly.

Difficulty: Difficult—really, this is quite difficult

Size: Best in pairs

Materials: Flipcharts; large and small Post-its

Don't do this in groups of more than four people.

Context: Good to start before or at the beginning of the sprint to explore the problem space before attempting to solve.

Approximate time: 15–20 minutes to start (can take longer depending on the size and nature of the project)

Credit: Min Basadur

DRIVE MORE BUSINESS for our CMRS?

OUR BIZ NESS!

HMW...
INCREASE CMR VALUE ↑ PROFITIBILITY

HMW...
INCREASE OUR CMRS MKT SAVVY

HMW...
GET THEM TO MARKET their BIZ MORE

HMW...
INCREASE OUR CMR SUCCESSES?

HMW...
FREE UP OUR CMRS TIME?

HMW...
MAINTAIN CMRS LONGER?

HMW...
PROVIDE MORE EDUCATION IN BUSINESS?

HMW...
GENERATE LEADS for OUR CMRS?

HMW...
MAKE things SIMPLER? (for them)

HMW...
CONNECT OUR CUSTOMERS IN A RELEVANT MANNER?

HMW...
MAKE THEM AWARE of EACH OTHER?

HMW...
DEFINE WHAT IS RELEVANT for THEM?

HMW...
IDENTIFY the RIGHT CONNECTIONS?

HMW...
NAVIGATE LEGAL LANG..? for T+C's

HMW...
TEST WHATS RELEVANT in a CONNXN?

HMW...
MINE OUR DATA TO LEARN THIS?

HMW...
GET OUT OF OUR OWN FUCKIN' WAY?

HMW..
HIJACK BIG DATA!

Know the User

In order to be successful, it is important to understand all the stakeholders surrounding a project, product, or service.

Regardless of what anyone else says, people are the ones to buy and use your product, so keep them at the center of your work. Personas are a good way to explore who those people are.

Personas are composite constructs of people, representations of the different types of people who use your product. They may be imaginary but they are not fictional, as they are based on knowledge of your customer base and/or user base. Personas are less about demographic data, and more about context, attitude, and behavior. If you already have personas from past work, that's excellent. You can bring the group up to speed and double-check that your assumptions are correct. If you don't have personas yet, that's OK; this is a great time to investigate the *who* you're solving for.

That said, it's important to define the difference between a user, a customer, and a persona. It's probably obvious, but to be clear, the user is a person who uses your product or service. A user might not be the person paying for or administering the product. A user may or may not be your customer. For example, a customer of

Google's AdWords may be the one setting up the ad (and paying for it), while another user may be a marketing director viewing the reports. Customers pay you money. Users use your product. They may be one and the same, but that's not always the case. Further, when you have multisided markets, as is common in marketplace apps like Airbnb or Lyft, you have multiple user types (i.e., multiple whos!).

The Who/Do exercise (from our friends who wrote *Gamestorming*) is a great way to begin to explore the stakeholder ecosystem. It answers two simple questions: *who* are the different stakeholders and what do you want to them to *do* with your product?

Once you know who the stakeholders are, you can flesh out more of the information about them. You won't have to consider all the stakeholders from the Who/Do exercise—one (or two) will suffice.

Who/Do

How

1. Draw a two-column table with "Who" on the left and "Do" on the right.

2. Ask the group: Who are the stakeholders? Who might be an obstacle? Whose support is critical to this project's success? Generate an exhaustive list of whos, writing each on the whiteboard or on a Post-it.

3. The Do column is typically more challenging. For each who, ask: What do they need to do, or do differently? What do they need to do for this project to be successful?

4. If necessary, you can add columns—for example, "Gives" and "Gets."

5. You can then rank and prioritize. If the choice isn't obvious, you can have each participant indicate the most important whos/dos by sticking dots on them.

Difficulty: Easy

Size: Teams or pairs

Materials: Sharpies; large and small Post-its in a variety of colors; wall or display board (horizontally oriented); dot stickers (optional)

Context: Good when first examining stakeholders of a project/product. Empathy maps, personas, and user stories or job stories are natural follow-ons.

Don't always drive toward action, as there is a tendency to say, "we just want them to understand." Ask the group, "What will happen when they understand?"

Approximate time: 10–30 minutes

Credit: Dave Grey at XPLANE

WHO

DO

SAVVY ANGEL → REVIEW FINANCE "DUE DILIGENCE?" | REVIEW SITE / TEAM |

GET EXCITED → SHARE // TELL SOMEONE
POST ON FBK / TWITTER

ANGEL FUND MANAGER → INVITE to APPLY for ..... | ENDORSE
RECOMMEND to COLLEAGUES |
VETTING PROCESS ... WHAT IS MONEY F
SETUP FOLLOW UP PITCH

SUCCESSFUL ENTREPRENEUR
└ KNOW ANGEL

LAWYER (REP's ANGELS) → SAME AS SAVVY

F.F.F. → RECOMMENDS | ENDORSES
SENDS EMAIL to ANGEL
SEE — ANGEL FU

Pay to the order of ___

AGREE to

Personas

Now that you know who your most important stakeholders are, you can go deeper into their personas. This will humanize your users and give the product team a sense of empathy for the people they're designing and developing for.

How

1. Do a quick recap of all the user information you have, both qualitative and quantitative (Discovery Interviews, site analytics, market research, etc.).

2. Categorize your personas with some or all the following information:

   a. Persona category (i.e., information seeker)

   b. Name (fictional names are often used, but sometimes using the first name of a real customer/user can help humanize further)

   c. Job titles and major responsibilities

   d. Backstory (demographics such as age, education, ethnicity, and family status; also include their physical, social, and technological environment)

   e. Motivations (the goals and tasks they are trying to complete using the site)

   f. Quote (this sums up what matters most to the persona as it relates to your product; preferably a real quote obtained during a Discovery Interview)

   g. Images (photographs and images representing this user group)

Difficulty: Moderate

Size: Entire group (if more than five people are in the room, split into teams)

Materials: Sharpies; flipcharts; wall or display board (horizontally oriented)

Context: If you do not have preexisting personas, a great place to start is a Who/Do exercise and then base personas from the selected whos. Combine that with any data from your market research, and other primary Discovery Interviews to create a composite.

Don't talk about a product or solution yet. Talk in abstractions. In addition, don't add aspects to a persona that aren't based on real-world research—just consider their world and what they're trying to get done.

Approximate time: 30–60 minutes, depending on depth of data you have

Credit: Alan Cooper is considered the pioneer of personas

"ALLEN"

MKTG MGR @ RIKER-G◯ (A PR FIRM)

MKT SAVVY ———————————————— X

TECH SAVVY —————————— X ···········X

TIME ———————— X

FRUSTRATIONS

NEW CATEGORIES OF BIZ
"UNFAMILIAR"

WANNABE MKTG FIRMS

MULTIPLE VARYING CLIENTS

CONSTANTLY EVOLVING TOOLS
(TECH)

NEEDS + WANTS

TO FIND NEW CHANNELS
for CLIENTS

TO ~~PROVE~~ PROVE VAL
JUSTIFY FEES

METRICS ⎍⎍⎍ SUCC
STO

TO STAY "ON BRAND"

JOBS · TO · BE · DONE

EFFICIEN MKR $ d for CLIENTS

Discovery Interview

This is the first part of the design sprint where the team will get to talk to users and/or customers...you know: people! Research you may already have on hand will tell you the what and when of a user's actions, but the why remains elusive and the best way is to converse directly with an actual user to discover this information, and any other relevant information that may help drive the design of a product or service.

As an example, when Dana Mitroff-Silvers began a design sprint for the Denver Museum of Nature and Science, she started by running all the participants through an introductory "wallet project" design-thinking exercise from Stanford's d.school:[7]

"It's essentially the wallet exercise from the Stanford d. school, but I change it out every time with a different design challenge based on where I'm going and who the group is. We've designed a morning commute. We designed the ideal neighborhood. We designed a Sunday night experience. It all depends on who I'm working with."

By completing this exercise up front, she was able to navigate the remainder of the sprint and refer back to it to reinforce its concepts as necessary during the rest of the sprint, ultimately bringing a sense of empathy to the team. After the introductory exercise, she sent everyone out into the museum to observe and interact with museum goers:

"We get ready to go out and do the real interviews; we talk about what the design challenge is, and then we talk about questions you might ask. Sometimes I let people draft their own questions; sometimes I give them starter questions. It depends on how much time and the group's comfort level and then I send them off to do interviews. Sometimes we do some observation of museum visitors out in the gallery: "What are they doing? What are they using? What kind of figures are you seeing?"

Larissa Chavarria at The Advisory Board does something similar: although she doesn't have the luxury that the museum has with a location full of users to access, she has her teams get on the phone with users. Because of the nature of their product, sometimes users are internal employees and there's easier access, but for many teams, scheduling interviews on short notice is a challenge.

---

7 The Wallet Exercise is 90-minute project through a full design cycle. Participants gain an experiential introduction to the phases of the design approach and some shared vocabulary. (*http://bit.ly/wallet-proj*).

"After each interview, the team gets together and does a team debrief. After every interview, we have sticky notes, and it's two minutes to write down, 'what do you think the user really wanted or what was surprising?' Having the sticky notes helps people who are maybe more introverted or some people who are stronger at the table can sort of overpower a meeting. The sticky note process is great because everyone silently brainstorms. You put them up on the wall and you say, 'OK, this is a recurring theme. You group those together. This is an outlier, we didn't think about it.' Then you vote, 'do you think this is important? Or is this a totally random thought?' It's a good process to make everyone equal."

Once they have completed the interviews, her team creates a matrix to determine which observations are important to drive the next phase.

Conducting a Discovery Interview is a great way to delve deeper into the context of the problem. We encourage video and audio recordings of these whenever possible so that the entire team can hear the customers' own words.

How

1. Create a brief description (up to two sentences) of a goal of what you seek to learn.
2. Select some icebreaker questions—something that will build rapport with the interviewee. Remember: They are a human, too!
3. Make a topic map rather than specific questions.
4. Have one person ask the questions where possible. Let the user focus on them. Downplay the other people present.
5. After an introduction, briefly describe the reason for the interview, and work through the topic map.
6. Thank them and ask for their email address (to follow up with a thank-you note!)

Difficulty: Difficult

Size: Best in pairs, but if users are in limited supply, the whole team can listen in

Materials: A/V recorder; notepad and pen; camera; topic map; users to talk to

Context: Best on the first day of the design sprint after everyone's received a data-dump and has completed the earlier exercises.

Don't talk more than you listen, or ask leading questions.

Approximate time: 15–30 minutes per interview; 60 minutes total (or longer if the schedule allows)

User Journey Map

Now that you've gotten to know the user, you'll want to look from a holistic viewpoint at what the users are doing before, during, and after the time they use your product. This will add context to your project and highlight opportunities you may have otherwise missed. We often see teams focusing only on areas where the customer is engaged in using the product, and they miss out on many opportunities to create delightful experiences based on that behavior or entry point.

Using an experience map or a user journey map is an excellent way to visualize the journey. In a user journey map, you break down the journey of each persona into different stages. Once you have all of those stages (and goals for each stage), you can see the touchpoints where the user would interact with your product or service. "Touchpoints" are the interactions of personas with the product or service. Keep in mind that the different personas you created earlier may have different needs, attitudes, and behaviors—however, their journeys may remain the same. They might not, hence the need for this journey map.

Let's consider a search engine optimization (SEO) example. Before a user is thinking about SEO, she is writing content for her blog, creating marketing collateral, or perhaps responding to a review on Yelp. Maybe she's taking a call from a customer or writing an email in response to a support ticket. All these activities can yield insight into how you might engage users who are undertaking SEO activities. Understanding the user's situation is key to defining the context and the opportunities your team has to create a solution that not only meets, but also delights.

A journey map documents the stakeholder experience from beginning to end, inside and outside of the product to identify opportunities for ideation. Further, the team will keep the waystations on the user's journey map in mind as they sketch their ideas during the Diverge phase of the design sprint.

How

1. Divide group into smaller teams according to the number of key stakeholders or personas you are completing journey maps for.

2. Each team defines the stages of the current stakeholder experience from beginning to end on large Post-its in a horizontal line at the top of the wall or display board.

3. For each stage, define the goal(s) the stakeholder has for that stage; write these on small Post-its, one goal per Post-it, and place directly beneath the corresponding stage.

4. Continue this process for tasks and tools.

5. Next, map the stakeholder mental state by either drawing a moving line(s) across all the stages (high = happy, low = unhappy) or by noting significant points of mental state with happy or sad faces, or the corresponding emotion label (e.g., relieved).

6. Based on low points on the mental state, list needs, then opportunities, on small Post-its, one need/opportunity per Post-it, and post below the corresponding stage.

7. If necessary, perform a vote (using dot stickers) to determine primary opportunities to move forward with.

Difficulty: Moderate

Size: Teams

Materials: Sharpies, large and small Post-its in a variety of colors, wall or display board (horizontally oriented), dot stickers (optional)

Context: Good to do after background activities and before ideation activities. It's not necessary to complete every level of analysis for all journey maps. Choose the analysis points that meet the needs of each design sprint. It's best that journey maps focus on existing workflows, but they can be modified to map out proposed goals and needs to define what should be built.

Don't just focus on the product workflow; you'll want to include product elements that are part of the user's current path that does not involve interaction with the product. Don't leave out the user's mental state, as this is a significant eye-opener.

Approximate time: 60–90 minutes

Credit: Various sources

Patient Experience Map
Yakima Valley Farm Workers Clinic

Phase	Triggering event and pre-event	Choose/schedule care	Apply for benefits
Channel	Radio, TV, billboards, word-of-mouth	Social, phone, web, word-of-mouth	Patient benefits coordinator
New Patient	Heart attack · ER · Rehabilitation · Released from rehab & urged to seek a primary physician.	Research · Calls multiple providers · Scheduled · **Danger Zone:** Poor customer service can permanently lose a current or potential patient.	Referred to patient benefits coordinator · Established as cash pat
Established Patient	Positive pregnancy test	Call · Scheduled	
Trust (High / Low)	We know the YVFWC has a good reputation in the community and can reasonably expect to start out with a high level of trust	If time is only available in the distant future trust can erode quickly and completely.	Benefits paperwork should be comparable anywhere, but the PBCs can gain trust here.
Thinking Feeling Doing Saying Seeing Hearing	**Doing:** Going to community events sponsored by clinic. **Hearing:** Peers talk about clinic. **Thinking:** "I can trust them." **Seeing:** Friends/family are getting treated affordably.	**Doing:** Asking others about clinics. Making calls to a few clinics. **Saying:** "I'm too busy." **Thinking:** "I don't have time to go to the doctor, but my family needs me to be well."	**Doing:** Applying for Medicaid or ACA. **Thinking:** "This paperwork is overwhelming" "Do I actually qualify for benefits"
Pain Points	• Patient has no care history. • Patient has care history with a different provider.	• Scheduling: personal availability, availability of providers or locations. • Problems are potentially more urgent than patient is willing to state.	• High volume of paperwork. • Difficulty in applying for coverag • Can't pay for care. • Lack of identification, fluidity in naming conventions, name chan

it for appointment		Appointment day	Follow-up
inder in mail		In-person	Phone, mail

New patient wait time is usually from
to 4 weeks depending on many factors.

Reminder card received

Patient checks in — **Seen by provider**

Waiting & paperwork — Checked out & given pay options

Payment follow up?

Care plan follow through depends on patient and their family.

anger Zone:
long wait for an appointment increases the chances
a patient finding another provider, cancelling, or not
owing up.

Danger Zone:
Long waits can create negative sentiment.

tient may be seen in as little as one day
f established and on a treatment plan.

Reminder card received

Patient checks in — **Seen by provider**

Waiting & paperwork — Checked out & given pay options

Payment follow up?

Future appointments determined by care plan established with provider.

onger a patient has to wait to be seen, ower trust can drop.	Again, there's a lot of room to lose trust here, but the quality of care YVFWC offers can put it on the higher end.	The quality of follow up contact provides a lot of opportunities, to build trust and to build habits of healthy living and care.

g: ng. dition may be changing, for better or for worse. **king**: n't wait so long to see a doctor." y does it take so long to be seen?" better, I don't need to keep my appointment."	**Doing**: Filling out additional paperwork. Getting benefits counseling. Getting treatment. Paying or deferring to benefits. **Thinking**: "Why do I have to wait so long?" "The care here is really good."	**Doing**: May or may not be keeping up with care plan. May ignore follow up communication. May never receive follow up communication. **Thinking**: "Do I really have to stick to this?" **Saying**: "They took really good care of me."

ient gets sicker while waiting. ient finds another clinic. ient talks themself out of seeing a doctor. mpeting priorities.	• Long clinic wait times. • Transportation difficulties. • Patient shows up late (won't be seen). • Provider is running behind. • Clinic is overscheduled.	• Missing or incorrect contact details.

Daily Retrospective (Plus/Delta)

What have we learned? We've taken the data we have and considered those constraints. We've spent all the energy and effort up to this point understanding and identifying the problem. This is a good time to take a step back to reflect on your work and appreciate what was accomplished, and allow everyone to propose improvements and share concerns, and plan action items.

The end of the day is an ideal time to do a retrospective, even if that falls in the middle of one of the design sprint phases. It's a great way for the team to come together before everyone leaves for the night, giving closure to the day by reflecting on it and planning for tomorrow.

There are many common retrospective formats. We recommend a Plus/Delta approach.

How
1. Draw two columns on a whiteboard: one for a "+" (plus: what went well) and one for "Δ" (delta: the Greek symbol for change).
2. Ask the group to reflect on what was positive and capture those thoughts under the "+" column.
3. Ask the group then to candidly brainstorm what they would change about the day, and put these under the "Δ" column.
4. For each item in the "Δ" column, list any action items that can be taken. For example, "revisit the challenge statement to include Larissa's feedback about older users." Address these action items in the next day's activities, or note them for future sprints.

Difficulty: Easy

Size: Everyone

Materials: Whiteboard or Post-its

Context: Done at the end of every phase, except the Prototype phase, which requires a longer, more in-depth retrospective of the entire design sprint.

Don't ignore or skip over this exercise; daily reflection will help you continually monitor your progress. Don't think that every delta is an immediate action item, or allow deltas to become just "what I didn't like."

Approximate time: 10–15 minutes at the end of each day, 30 minutes at the end of the design sprint

Credit: Plus/Deltas are found in the book *Gamestorming*. The earliest known use of the Plus/Delta game is at The Boeing Co circa 1980.

GOOD!

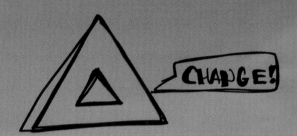
CHANGE!

+ GOOD!	△ CHANGE!

GOOD! (+)

- Realisation of Volume of work
- CUPCAKES
- I CAN APPLY THIS TO MY DAY-TO-DAY WORK
- GIVING STRATEGY INPUT
- Awareness
- + Participation Rate
- THE DEDICATED TIME TO COLLABERATE
- GOOD TO COLLABORATE
- Time investment is worth it

CHANGE! (△)

- △ Teams
- DO IT MORE. DO IT EARLIER.
- DO IT MORE
- DO IT BIGGER (TOPICS)
- FOCUS Narrower
- DID WE HAVE ENOUGH TIME FOR 4 AREAS OF FOCUS?
- BETTER EXPLANATION OF DAY IN ADVANCE
- TRAIN ME TO DELIVER THIS SESSION.

Team Drinks: Less Filling and Tastes Great!

As the first day concludes, take the opportunity to go out with the team if you can. Getting out of the conference room will give you a fresh perspective, and the conversations you have will forge connections with your colleagues that will last the duration of your project and beyond. You will likely be tired toward the end of the remaining days of your sprint, so take advantage of this.

Drinks are a low-pressure way to get together without a big time commitment. The people who are local will then be able to get home to their families at a reasonable hour. Make sure you leave early enough; we prefer to leave for drinks no later than 4:30 p.m. (or 5 p.m. at the latest). If people want to spend more time after, anyone who chooses to can go out to dinner.

If there isn't a good place to go nearby, raid the beer and soda fridge and have a chat in your company's lounge or café. It's almost as good, and you can't beat the price!

Pace yourself; the second day of a design sprint is coming up soon and will be an intense one. Equally attractive nonalcoholic beverages (EANABs) are also always an option!

How

You need instructions for this?

1. Go forth and get drinks!
2. Enjoy.

Takeaways:

- Inspire yourselves with background materials and other solutions to similar and related problems.

- Define the problem and take time to understand it and the data you currently have about it.

- List out all your assumptions, facts, and remaining questions that your current data and research do not answer.

- Conduct Discovery Interviews so your team can understand who they're designing for.

- Create personas to humanize your users. They are people too!

- Map out the user's current journey or experience so you have a full visual context of the problem at hand. You'll be able to identify which areas to focus on creating a solution or a fix to a current friction point.

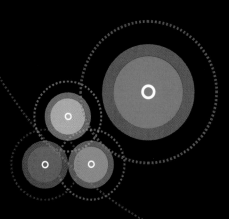

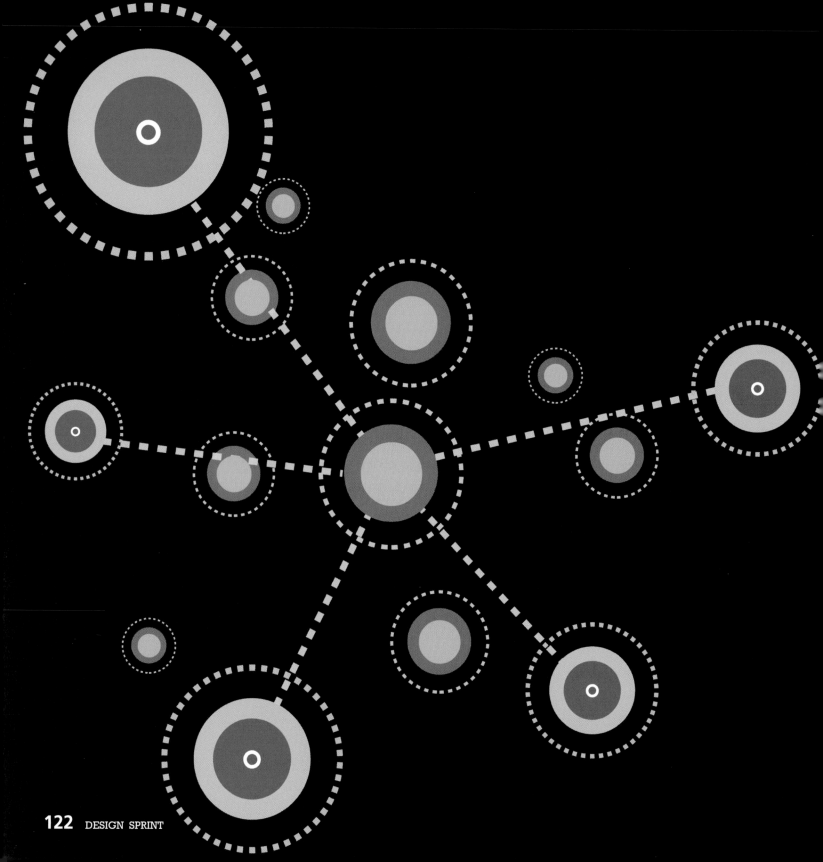

Chapter 6

Phase 2: Diverge

Now that we have an initial understanding of the users and a problem of theirs worth solving, it's time to look at potential solutions, generating as many ideas as possible. Don't think of this as group brainstorming. Rather, it's about each person working individually to sketch their ideas without the pressures of groupthink, then sharing them with the rest of the group, using the wisdom of the crowd to vote for the best ideas. The focus of the Diverge phase is to explore the range of possibilities. The exercises described in this chapter are designed to get the ideas out of your head and onto paper or the whiteboard. There are also many other types of divergent exercises. We present those that have worked best for us in a design sprint, but there are many others that can fit just fine.

In our experience, the Diverge phase is the most exhilarating and the most exhausting. At the end of it, you'll feel a lot of confusion over having so many options and not knowing which to choose. That's normal—trust the process: the Converge phase that follows will guide you to the right options to explore and test further.

At Constant Contact, the Diverge phase often brings participants from other areas of the company into the project for their input. This allows a couple of things to happen: first, the additional brainpower and different viewpoints can act as a way to further challenge ideas and push them to be better, as they bring a fresh perspective. Second, by inviting others in the organization to participate, you help evangelize the framework and the mindset. Over time, more and more Constant Contact employees participated in some part of the design sprint process, and it even reached a point where members of the executive team were advocating the approach on a number of initiatives in the company.

What Happens During the Diverge Phase?

Gear Up	~1 hour
Generate Solutions	~2 hours
Generate More Solutions	~2 hours (optional)
Individual Wireframes	~1 hour (optional)

You'll notice that there are two Generate stages here. It's worth noting that not every Diverge phase will require multiple Generate stages. Your group might be able to generate enough great ideas in the first round. Cycling through multiple Generate stages is very useful when you have a small group. Larger groups by their nature will generate larger collections of ideas, and need more time to review them together. Smaller groups might need one or two more Generate cycles to get to a critical mass of ideas. Each time the cycle is repeated, the group will get more familiar with the exercises and it will become easier to repeat them.

We also have individual wireframing listed as optional because it's not always necessary. Wireframes are useful but if the solution you're designing includes some experiential or service elements, it will be more relevant to sketch those activities in storyboards rather than describing just the interactions with the screens in the wireframes.

Because the purpose of the Diverge phase is to generate a lot of ideas, any exercises that can do that will be useful. You might want to do other idea-generation exercises that aren't listed here, and that's OK. Or you might find that you want to do fewer or more rounds of Crazy Eights or storyboards. Take advantage of the flexibility of the design sprint framework as you modify it to meet your needs, and again feel free to extend, shorten, or skip exercises as needed.

Time constraints are a key part of today's work, so repeat the Diverge or Extend cycles to the amount of time you have allotted for the day. These exercises will be intense! Continue to take the breaks you need to get the most out of them.

Recommended Agenda

Gear Up

Review Agenda and Rules	~5 minutes
Pitch Practice (Chapter 5)	~5 minutes
Background Phase Recap	~20 minutes
Job Stories	~30 minutes

Generate Solutions (At least once; 1–2 more times are optional)

Mind Map	~10 minutes
8-Ups (aka Crazy Eights)	~10 minutes
Storyboard	~20 minutes
Silent Critique	~10 minutes
Group Critique	~3–5 minutes per person
Super Vote (Optional)	~5 minutes

Generate More Solutions (Optional)

8-Ups (aka Crazy Eights)	~10 minutes
Storyboard	~20 minutes
Silent Critique	~10 minutes
Group Critique	~3–5 minutes per person
Super Vote (Optional)	~5 minutes

Individual Wireframes (Optional)

Wireframe Storyboard	~30 minutes
Silent Critique	~10 minutes
Group Critique	~3–5 minutes per person

Wrap-up

Daily Retrospective	~15 minutes

Gear Up

To get ready to explore a broad range of ideas, you'll first want to set the stage. Because of the amount of background you've all just seen, it's important to touch on the most important points. That way you'll start from a position of clarity with a brief review of the problem you're solving, who you're solving it for, and what they need to get done.

This quick review of how the prior day went will help you take advantage of the connections our brains can create while we're asleep, which can lead to "aha" moments. According to a 2007 study at the University of California Berkeley, upon waking from sleep, people are 33% more likely to make connections between seemingly distantly related ideas.[1] So your ideas about goat cheese roller skates may prove useful after all!

---

1   Jeffrey M. Ellenbogen, Peter T. Hu, Jessica D. Payne, Debra Titone, and Matthew P. Walker, "Human Relational Memory Requires Time and Sleep," PNAS vol. 104, no. 18 (2007): 7723-7728.

Review Agenda and Rules

As before, tell the team what's about to happen. As you move into idea generation, make sure people feel comfortable so that they can speak their mind and stay engaged.

We have seen some teams run warm-up exercises at the beginning of the Diverge phase, and that can be fun. It can be good to shake things up and get everyone doing something unrelated, especially if people seem sluggish. However, if the team is ready to go, then skip the warm-up exercise and get right into the action!

How

1. Review the printed agenda for the Diverge phase, or bring it up on a large TV screen.
2. In about a sentence each, describe the exercises you'll be doing together.
3. Reinforce to the group that the Diverge phase is about generating ideas and that there are no right or wrong answers.
4. Review the rules you discussed the day before, adding or removing any if needed.
5. Optional: Do a warm-up exercise, like Word Ball, as described in Chapter 5.

Difficulty: Easy

Size: The whole group

Materials: Printed agenda or a TV screen

Don't go into detail.

Approximate time: 5 minutes

Background Phase Recap

There will have been a lot of discussions during the background phase, and the amount of information can be overwhelming. Some people might have stepped out or tuned out during a key conversation, or forgotten it overnight after a lively team outing! A quick review on what was discussed the prior day will bring conversations back to keep them fresh.

How

1. Review the goals, personas, challenge statement, and user journey map you created. Take turns: ask different people to present each one by reading or summarizing it aloud.
2. Ask the group to mention any other key points that stuck in their minds.

Difficulty: Easy

Size: Entire group

Don't reinitiate previous debates.

Approximate time: 15–20 minutes

Job Stories

As you prepare to leave the background discussions behind and sketch solutions, you'll want to ensure that the users and their problems are your first priority. A great way to do that is with job stories.

Job stories have a fill-in-the-blank format. Remember the Mad Libs you did as a kid? (Or still do them now? We do!) A job story is a user-centered Mad Lib, where you get to fill in the situation of what can happen to a user, as well as the user's motivations and desired outcomes.

Focus on the problems that users have, and the "job" the products they "hire" solve for. You're still focused on the problem—we'll get to create solutions later.

How

1. Start with the high-level task or job the user is attempting to accomplish.
2. Break that job down into smaller tasks, or smaller jobs.
3. For these smaller jobs, discuss how users solve the problem now. Craft one or more job stories that investigate the causality, anxieties, and motivations of what they do now:
   a. On a large Post-it, write: When _____, I want to _____, so that _____.
   b. Fill in the blanks: When _(event happens)_, I want to _(motivation or desire)_, so that _(outcome)_.
4. Have each team share their job stories with the group.

Difficulty: Moderate

Size: Teams or pairs

Materials: Post-its and pens

Don't focus on the feature; don't forget about the why.

Approximate time: 30–60 minutes

Credit: Alan Klement[2]

---

2 Alan Klement, "Replacing the User Story with the Job Story," November 12, 2013. *http://bit.ly/klement-story.*

Generate Solutions

When starting an idea-generation exercise, begin by letting each individual work alone, then proceed to share ideas with the group. This will allow everyone to think in their own way about the problem, enabling their brains to deconstruct and reconstruct a model of the information that works for them. Doing so lets each person generate ideas while keeping someone else's mental constructs from overpowering them. Now that you've identified some constraints in all the background exercises, you'll want to unleash as much creative freedom as possible.

Once everyone has had time to consider the problem and generate their own possible solutions, sharing with the group will allow the participants to riff on one another's ideas, building and expanding upon them. Excessive criticism of ideas at this stage is particularly detrimental to Diverge phase objectives and sprint process goals. That is why the Converge phase exists, and we'll get to that in the next chapter. Diverge is all about generating as many ideas as you can—sometimes the more crazy and removed from reality, the better. If you're as crazy as us (you're reading this book, so we presume you are) you'll have no problem.

At this stage, the goal is quantity, not necessarily quality. Ira Glass, the famous story-teller heard on *This American Life* once spoke about how doing a quantity of work early in your career helps you get better at whatever you do. A similar concept applies here. You will rarely come up with "the big idea" immediately. However, you will generate multiple ideas or even iterations of those ideas. It costs very little to generate and iterate on ideas, but once you start executing and bringing them to life, things can get costly, so go for quantity at this point. In C. Todd's Creativity and Innovation class at IE Business School, he forces his MBA student teams to generate at least 100 ideas for the problem they are solving. Justin Lloyd, a lecturer at the Maryland Institute College of Art, spoke about how his graphic design professors forced him to generate 500 different concepts of a logo design for his class projects. Quantity helps to bring out the quality. While you may hit on a flash of inspiration, these are incredibly rare. There are no shortcuts, so get to grinding, ideating, and iterating in order to see the fruits of your labor. As we said earlier, you might need to cycle through the Generate stage more than once to produce enough useful ideas. All three of us have seen scenarios where one cycle was sufficient, but we've often needed to run through the exercises twice or more to get enough ideas to work with. We don't believe there is a magic number of ideas, but we do know that the more ideas you generate, the more opportunities for solutions will be created.

These don't have to be your original ideas either—they can be ideas from others in the company, the group, or elsewhere. Your ideas will start to come to life when you get them out on paper. Drawing them on paper democratizes the process, because anyone can draw. Yes, you—you can draw! Can you write the alphabet? We bet you can! If you can do that, you can draw all sorts of lines and shapes. Using thicker pens such as Sharpies ensures the fidelity stays low so it forces you to be clear and also forgives any squiggly lines.

In most design sprints, you'll get to go through two or more cycles of idea generation. Therefore, it's useful to limit the scope of each cycle by breaking the user journey map into two or more pieces. If there's a single user journey, a good way to do this is to break it in half, and focus your initial idea-generation cycle around the most important half of the user journey, and the next cycle on the other half.

If there are two primary user types (e.g., educators and learners or buyers and sellers), that can be a good way to break up the user journey as well. You can generate ideas for the most important users first, and the additional users later. If it makes sense to break the user's journey up into more than two chunks, you'll need to make time for additional iterations of the idea-generation cycle, or shorten each cycle.

Mind Map

To ease into the generation of ideas, it's important to let everyone first collect their thoughts. There doesn't need to be much rhyme or reason to how they do it; what's important is that they do it.

A great way to get started is with mind mapping. There is no right or wrong way to create a mind map—it is a representation of a participant's mental model of a particular topic.

Have everyone write down or draw everything that they are thinking about. Keep the format free so that people feel comfortable to explore any and all ideas. You can draw people, screens, words, or anything. If the thing you drew triggered another thought, you can link them together, but you don't have to. What you draw is up to you.

How

1. Review the user journey map from the Understand phase, and select the part of the user journey you want to focus on first. Again, this often is the first half of the user's journey, or the journey of just one user type if there are multiple user types.
2. Give everyone a few sheets of paper and Sharpies.
3. Start sketching words, pictures, users, screens, or ideas. Have everyone write down or draw everything that they are thinking about.
4. These can be connected to other ideas, but don't have to be.
5. Keep the ideas flowing. It doesn't matter what you write or draw, as long as you keep writing and drawing.

Difficulty: Easy
Size: Individuals
Materials: Pen and paper

Don't rush, or feel you're doing it wrong. Don't let writer's block set in and stare at a blank page.

Approximate time: 10 minutes

Credit: British psychologist Tony Buzan popularized the mind map in the 1960s.

8-Ups (AKA Crazy Eights)

Now that you're warmed up with some ideas on paper, it's time to generate many more, and start to build on one another's ideas. We do this with a structured sketching exercise, where you have 30 seconds each to sketch eight different ideas, each in a separate frame on an 8.5 × 11 piece of paper.

This can be the most intense and most enjoyable part of the design sprint, and again there aren't any right or wrong ways to sketch it. You might write down a few words, or sketch the user having a problem and interacting with the product to fix it, or draw a random screen from what the product might look like.

The fidelity can be quite low: the sketches don't need to mean anything to anyone but you just yet. No one will be reviewing these up close, so don't worry about what anyone will think.

What you draw can come from the mind maps you just did, or could be something completely new. They also don't have to have anything to do with each other or go in order; the sketches are a grab bag of ideas and we'll get the chance to string them together later.

All ideas are fair game: old ideas, new ideas, and the crazy ideas that pop up when you think there are no ideas left and you feel like you really have to reach. That's when you come up with something completely random that often ends up to be unexpectedly awesome. That's why this exercise is sometimes called Crazy Eights!

We recommend doing two cycles, going around the room quickly after each round to explain what you drew, so people can expand upon what you did in the next set of 8-Ups and the exercises to come.

How

1. Review the user journey map and highlight the part of the user journey you want to focus on.

2. Take a sheet of paper and fold into eight equal areas. In each fold, you'll want to fold the paper the fat way (landscape), not the thin (portrait) way. (One of thoughtbot's clients used to be an elementary school teacher, and described this way of folding as "Hamburger hamburger" to make the frames nice and fat, as opposed to "Hot dog hot dog" which would make them too thin!)

3. Set a timer for 5 minutes. We recommend using the BitTimer app on your phone, configured to 30 seconds of work, 10 seconds of rest, and 8 repetitions.

4. Every 40 seconds, draw a completely different solution to different aspects of the problem. The facilitator says when to begin, and announces every 40 seconds that it's time to move on to the next frame until all eight are filled in.

5. Share with the rest of group. Each person should take no more than 1 minute to describe their sketches in a few words each. In large groups of more than about six people, call out just the highlights so the descriptions take about 30 seconds. There isn't time yet to start a discussion or get feedback; you'll do that in a moment when you review each other's storyboards.

6. Repeat steps 1–5 one more time. You're encouraged to steal, modify, and expand upon each other's ideas!

Difficulty: Moderate

Size: Individually, then present to the group

Materials: A4, letter, or tabloid-sized paper for writing

Don't take too long on any one idea—keep moving on to the next ones! Don't start a discussion yet of any of the ideas.

Approximate time: 20–30 minutes (5 minutes to sketch, and 5–10 minutes to share with the group for each of two iterations)

Credit: Will Evans' Design Studio methodology,[3] the 6-8-5 exercise from *Gamestorming*,[4] Jake Knapp at Google Ventures.[5]

---

3 *http://bit.ly/intro-studio*

4 *http://www.gogamestorm.com/?p=688*

5 *http://www.gv.com/lib/the-product-design-sprint-divergeday2*

Storyboard

Now that you have a slew of rough ideas on paper at your fingertips, it's time to organize them just enough to show them to the group and get feedback. You'll do this by creating three storyboard frames for one or more of your best ideas, for a particular persona and job story or segment of the user journey. This will build off that scenario, bringing it to life by visualizing how a user would use your product at work or at play.

These are like frames from a comic book, or the storyboards people create when sketching out scenes for a movie. The three frames work best when they tell a story about a single interaction, but it's fine if it makes sense to instead have multiple interactions to showcase more great ideas.

It's preferable to show stick-figure style sketches of users in the situation where they need to get something done and your idea offers a good solution. A storyboard's best if it tells a story about real people! Still, if it will tell a better story to instead have a screen from your product, that's OK too. You'll get a chance to create your own wireframes later, at the end of the Diverge phase.

Once you've drawn your sketches, you'll then need to write out just a brief description of what's happening, so people can get a good sense of the situation you drew and what's happening. You'll review these all together in the exercises to come.

How

1. Again, briefly review part of the user journey map or the job story you want to focus on.
2. Stick three Post-its along the left side of a sheet of paper, leaving room for text on the right.
3. Draw out your scenario(s), considering human-human interactions, not just human-device interactions.
4. Add a small text caption to the right of each frame to describe what's happening.

Difficulty: Easy

Size: Individually

Materials: A4, letter, or tabloid-sized paper; Post-its

Don't include too many screens and not enough humans. Don't write too much text. Don't sign your name.

Approximate time: About 20 minutes

Credit: Disney artist and animator Webb Smith is credited with creating the first storyboard.

Teacher character guide

TEACHER CHARACTER GUIDE BOOK

(PRINT or WEB)

A two-week "Roll-out" guide, differentiated by grade level, in either print or online (like TB's PlayBook) Features daily lesson plans, read aloud books, student journal prompts, videos, station activities, class discussion prompts, etc. Could give kids opportunity to practice safely giving feedback to each other

→ cards

→ poster

ZEST!

↳ journal book

PRINT·BASED TOOLS for STUDEN[T]

Paper-based tools for students (approp[riate] by grade level) might include a set of character cards (w/ illustration on front + behaviors/ indicators on back), classroom posters, or a printed journal book that asks kids specific prompts ("Tell about a time you show[ed] grit... who in your family has the most self-control? why)" to introduce conce[pts]

take-home materials
↓

FAMILY INTRODUCTION NIGHT

Family night (classroom- or school- wide) to introduce concepts to families, talk about the tool, what

Silent Critique

Awesome, you now have your first storyboards! Celebrate by pinning or taping them up on the wall for the whole group to see. It's time for everyone to review each other's work and start highlighting the best ideas.

The easiest, fastest way to get everyone's initial feedback is to have the full group walk around the room and look at all the storyboards, indicating the things they like. Translucent green dot stickers work best so you can still see the work underneath when a lot of them are stuck to the best ideas. If you don't have green stickers, very small Post-its or even pen marks will do!

No one has their names on the storyboards that were created, and they're all being reviewed silently and at the same time. This levels the playing field, as ideas can be appreciated for their quality instead of how loudly and passionately they were presented and by whom. Project sponsors, startup CEOs, designers, developers, marketing, interns, subject matter experts—everyone gives and receives the same votes. There will soon be ample opportunities to discuss the merits of the ideas in the group critique.

How

1. Put everyone's storyboards up on the wall.
2. Hand out a sheet of stickers (preferably translucent green stickers) to the group.
3. Each person reads the storyboards, attaching green stickers to the storyboard frames whose ideas they think are best. You can vote for your own ideas, and there's no limit to how many stickers you can use.
4. Some ideas will start to stand out as they collect a cluster of stickers, creating a "heat map" of the most interesting ideas.

Difficulty: Easy

Size: The whole group, silently

Materials: Storyboards, walls, tape, and a slew of translucent green dot stickers

Don't be stingy with applying the stickers.

Approximate time: About 5–10 minutes, depending on the size of the group

Credit: The original source of the Dot Voting game is unknown. It's appeared in *Gamestorming*, Dotmocracy, and more recently in a Google Ventures post about Day 2 of a product design sprint.

Group Critique

Now that everyone has had a chance to review the storyboards and to quietly and quickly comment on them with their dot votes, you can now have a more in-depth discussion around the ideas presented. While the best storyboards are clear without any explanation, sometimes things aren't as clear as they could be and it helps to talk things through. This gives time for people to say what they thought was good about the ideas, and the people who created them can add more detail.

This design critique provides a collaborative process of presentation, critique, and iteration that leads to improved solutions. It's not a "design by committee," and should never be confused with it.

How

1. Have everyone gather around each storyboard.
2. Ask the group what they liked about the story-board.
3. Briefly go over any concerns if you wish.
4. Ask the person who created it if anything needs more explanation, giving them the opportunity to talk through it. They can feel free to pass if every-thing was clear.

Difficulty: Easy
Size: The whole group

Don't include only screenshots without telling the story. Don't write too much text.

Approximate time: About 3–5 minutes per person

Credit: Group critique has no single origin.

Super Vote (Optional)

With the benefit of everyone's explanations, it's time for another round of dot voting, with fewer stickers—"super votes" that call attention to the best ideas. This time, you'll want to reflect how decisions are made on your team by giving key stakeholders extra votes. When you reach the moment when you have your ideas ready, you can begin the voting process. Everyone gets a vote, which they can place next to the idea using a marker, sticker, or Post-it note. Colored stickers work very well. The idea/s with the highest number of votes will indicate the best concepts.

The super votes offer a unique way to tweak the process to reflect the decision-making structure of your team or company. Does your CEO make all final decisions about the product? If that's the case, be honest about it, and give her three super votes and everybody else one. Or maybe it's a UX director or maybe a tandem of product and design who call the shots. The simple rule is to give the deciders extra votes.

By default, this process will be a meritocracy, but that's not always the way companies work and, frankly, consensus can lead to poor design decisions. The last thing you want are decisions that the deciders don't truly support. On some teams, these may be unwritten rules, so don't be surprised if it feels a bit awkward to bring it up—in the long run, you'll be glad you did.

Right now, you're still generating ideas, and nothing's final yet. Just because an idea gets a lot of dot stickers or super votes doesn't necessarily mean that it will make it into what you decide during the Converge phase of the design sprint. There's still room for iteration and for other ideas to get prioritized.

In some design sprints, we've skipped this exercise as there's an opportunity for the key stakeholders to voice their opinions in the Converge phase. Some groups haven't wanted to emphasize this early in the sprint that certain people bear a greater part of the decision making. Still, a quick super vote exercise can be a good way to get a preview of possible decisions to come.

How

1. Give everyone one or two "super vote" dot stickers. These could be stickers of a different color, or the same green stickers with a pen mark on them.

2. Give key decision makers an extra two or three "super vote" dot stickers.

3. Have everyone attach their super vote stickers to the storyboards on the wall, as before.

Difficulty: Easy

Size: The whole group

Don't be afraid to give out dot stickers to key stakeholders.

Approximate time: About 5 minutes

Credit: Jake Knapp's post applied the super vote concept to dot voting, which again has unknown origin and was popularized in part by *Gamestorming*[6] and Dotmocracy.[7]

---

6 *http://www.gamestorming.com/core-games/dot-voting/*

7 *http://dotmocracy.org/*

Generate More (and More) Solutions

Whew—you've made it through your first idea-generation cycle. Go take a break!

Now that you're back and the team has gotten used to the rhythm of an idea-generation cycle, you'll want to repeat the cycle to generate more ideas. In the likely event that you focused on a part of the user journey, you can now focus on the rest. Or you might decide to limit the scope of the design sprint and just go deeper into the most important parts of the user interaction.

The idea-generation cycles get easier every time. And because everyone's warmed up, you don't have to do the mind maps the second time around: you can just go directly into the 8-Ups. The exercises are the same and we won't repeat them here. Now that you've found your groove, go do it again and generate more awesome ideas.

The agenda for your subsequent idea-generation cycles is as follows (we leave the mind maps out because they have already been completed and aren't something that's presented):

8-Ups (aka Crazy Eights)	~10 minutes
Storyboard	~20 minutes
Silent Critique	~10 minutes
Group Critique	~3–5 minutes per person
Super Vote (Optional)	~5 minutes

Individual Wireframes

As your last cycle of generating ideas, it can be useful for everyone present to create their version flow of the user's interaction through the product. Whereas the first part of the ideation work was more focused on users and their situations, problems, and jobs-to-be-done, now the focus is on the product itself.

The whole group doesn't have to get on the same page about the product yet. There will be time to do this in the Converge phase to come.

The cycle of the exercises you'll be doing is the same as before, except you'll review a full set of product wireframes instead of storyboards, and you won't need to do 8-Ups again as you'll have the full day's activities to serve as inspiration.

As such, here's the agenda for the wireframes iteration:

Wireframe	~30 minutes
Silent Critique	~10 minutes
Group Critique	~3–5 minutes per person

We marked the wireframes iteration as optional, as the group might not be ready to draw wireframes yet, or the time might be better spent continuing a regular iteration cycle with additional storyboards. Get a sense of whether the group's ready to tackle some individual wireframes, and if so, go for it!

Wireframes

Wireframes are rough sketches of the flow through the screens of your product. Note that the product may ultimately be comprehensive, but what you'll create will be a minimum viable version of that. As such, honor your timebox and don't spend more than 30 minutes sketching these out.

Don't worry about perfect user experience design of your screens just yet. You just want to focus on what the basic screens will do. At this stage, the fidelity of your sketches can be very low.

It's often useful to draw the wireframes on large Post-its, so you can mix and match everyone's screens when you assemble the full wireframes later during the Converge phase.

Also, it's best to focus on the happy path at this stage. Don't worry about edge or error cases yet. The idea is to capture what each person thinks the most likely main flow through the application will be.

How

1. Stick several large Post-its on several sheets of paper.
2. Draw out wireframes of all the user's interactions through the entire journey map.

Difficulty: Moderate to difficult

Size: Individually

Materials: A4, letter, or tabloid-sized paper; Post-its

Don't include edge cases or less important flows, or worry about perfect UX.

Approximate time: About 30 minutes

Credit: Wireframe illustrations date back as far as the Italian Renaissance. They were adapted electronically in the 1980s via computer-aided manufacturing techniques.

As you wrap up your day, be mindful of all the ideas you just created. This is often cited as the most fun part of the design sprint. You're able to think freely and creatively, and draw your ideas (See? You really did learn everything you needed to know in Kindergarten).

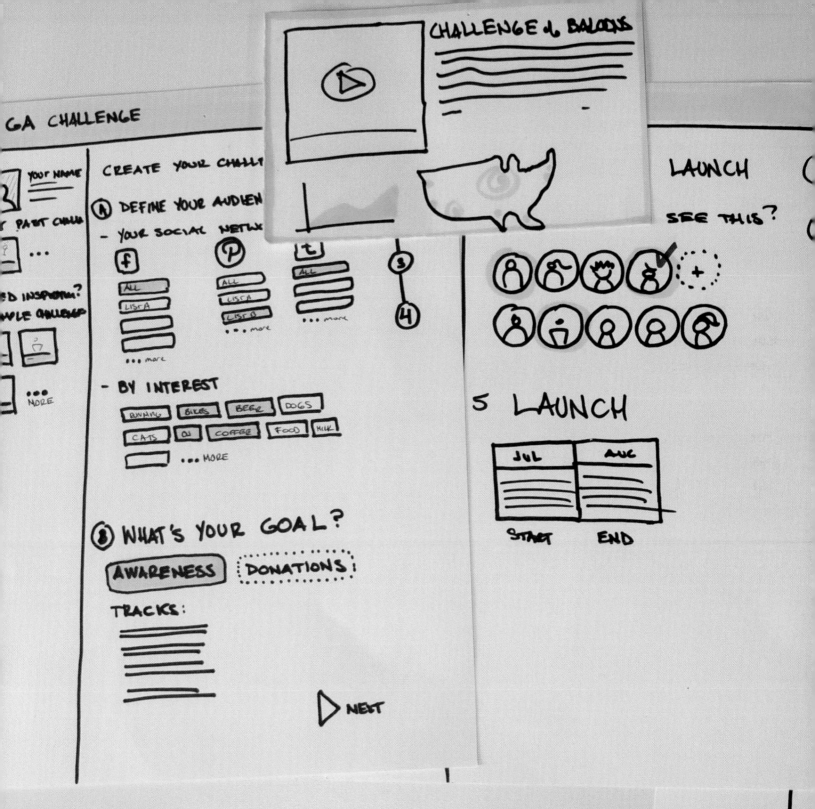

Takeaways:

- Generating ideas works best when focused on each individual's ideas, and not on group- generated ideas.

- Quantity is more important than quality while diverging. Quality will come later.

- Don't forget to dig into your backgrounds and introduce old ideas into the mix. Not all ideas need to be shiny and new.

- Repeating exercises is sometimes necessary to get enough ideas.

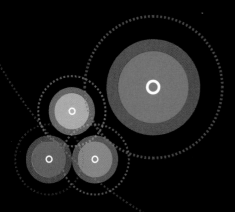

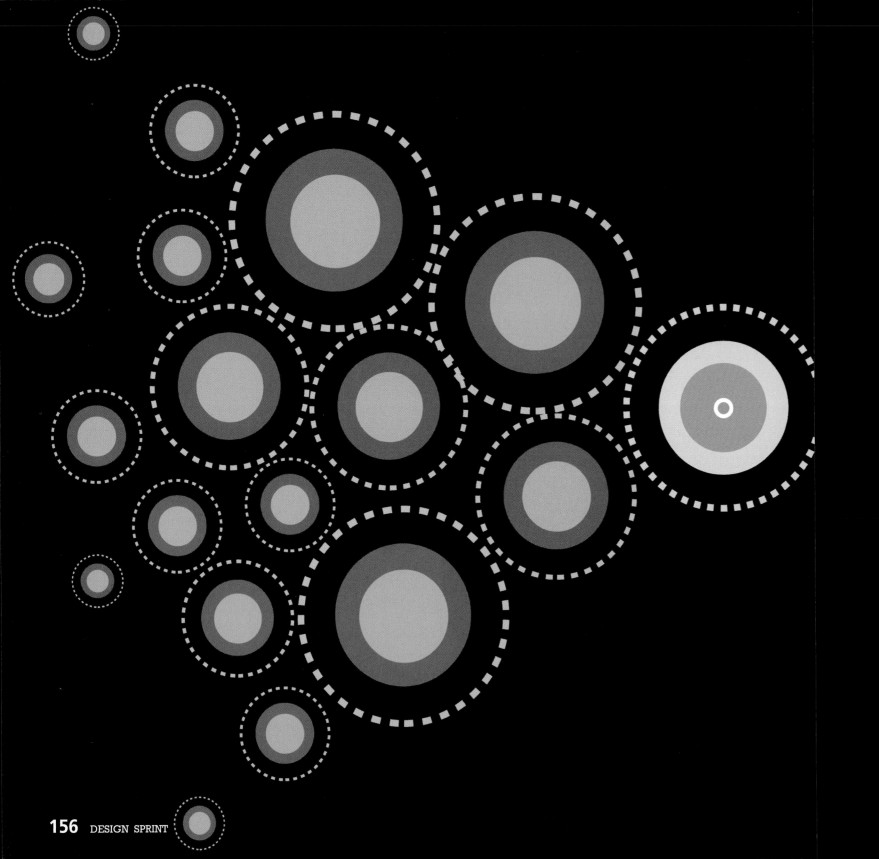

Chapter 7

Phase 3: Converge

It's now the middle of your design sprint: you've generated many ideas and it's time to start narrowing down the choices. The Converge phase does exactly that: it's about making hard choices and picking a direction to prototype and test with users.

You'll focus on having the right (and sometimes difficult) conversations about how you can solve your chosen problem, in order to design an effective solution. You will find yourselves debating frequently and perhaps heatedly. If everyone consistently agrees with everything, something is wrong.

At this point, you should have plenty of ideas to choose from so as much as you can, you'll want to winnow down what you already have rather than adding to an already large pile of broad possibilities.

ncluding all the voices in the room will give you the best possible insights from your team. Designers, developers, executives, customer service, and marketing folks will all bring different perspectives and solutions. Keep the conversation inclusive and open

It's important that the key stakeholders are in attendance when the most important decisions are made. If they're not able to attend the entire design sprint, have them attend this day. If they can't attend the entire day, have them present when you converge on the storyboard and wireframes. Ask that they not duck out for emails, calls, or meetings during these sessions. This way, they'll be part of the decisions. If they need to change anything for business reasons, they can provide that information right away while there's still time to make adjustments before the end of the design sprint, so they'll be less likely to require changes afterward.

What Happens During the Converge Phase?

Get Started	~30 minutes
Scrutinize Your Work	~3.5 hours
Sketch Final Wireframe	~3 hours

Recommended Agenda

Get Started

Describe the Converge Phase	~5 minutes
Pitch Practice (yes, again!)	~5 minutes

Scrutinize Your Work

Recap Background	~10 minutes
Review Assumptions	~45 minutes
$100 Test/Risks	~15 minutes
Identify Alternatives	~45 minutes
2x2 Matrix	~30 minutes (optional)

Wireframe the Prototype

Team Sketching	~25 minutes
Ritual Dissent	~5 minutes
Team Sketching	~25 minutes
Ritual Dissent	~5 minutes
Final Sketch	~2 hours

Wrap-up

Daily Retrospective	~15 minutes

As always, keep the flexibility of the design sprint process in mind. These exercises have worked well for us, but feel free to add, subtract, or replace exercises that you have experience with to help you meet your particular design sprint's goal.

Get Started

Dan Ramsden, Director of User Experience at the BBC, said it best in terms of a Darwinian theory:

"You've got to accept that some of your babies might be ugly. And you've got to kill them off so that you can concentrate on the nice ones. I suppose that discipline in a sprint is what makes it a really effective process because you haven't got the time to come up with excuses as to why this idea could work. It's like natural Darwinian design really. It's just like the fittest survive because you've only got a short amount of time. [When] we tried to cheat Darwin out of his theory, it didn't really work very effectively."

Robust debate is healthy for the design sprint process. If you have very divergent viewpoints, you'll get a better outcome. Let these viewpoints compete and don't seek too many compromises, and the results tend to be better.

At the same time, it's easy for shy or quiet people to be ignored or railroaded in these group activities. It's the role of the facilitator to be sensitive to the entire group's needs and include all opinions. Ask for individuals' contributions and beware of strong personalities that dominate conversations. We've seen this happen in almost all of the facilitated design sprints we've run. Don't let it happen to you.

Seth Godin, the prolific author and marketing guru, talks about embracing the generous skeptic who isn't shutting ideas out of fear, but is providing insight about something other people don't see yet.[1] He says,

---

1 *http://bit.ly/godin-skeptic*

"When the generous skeptic speaks up, she's taking a risk. If you respond to her generosity by arguing, by shutting down, by avoiding eye contact or becoming defensive, you've blown it. You've taken a gift and wasted it, and disrespected the gift giver at the same time...'Tell me more about that,' is the useful and productive response, not, 'no, you're wrong, you don't understand.'"

Similarly, Brian Colcord, Senior Director, UX and Product Design at LogMeIn, talks about being critical in design, saying:

"Critiquing is an art form. People think that feedback or, 'Hey, change this to this' is critiquing. That's not really what it's about. I'm not going to go to a business analyst and be like, 'Hey, I know this stuff better than you. Why are you not doing this?' This is where design sprints and design studios come in really nicely, to involve everybody in the process so that you're on the same page. You're understanding the direction, you're understanding the work that goes into what needs to get done."

He continues,

"I think in a critique it is important to be able to articulate what the problem is that you're seeing, based on something that's not your opinions. It's like I see a problem for this persona or this user or this particular principle that we have. Not saying, 'I think we should do this, because I think we should do this.' It's all about, 'Well this might not work here. Why did you make that decision?'"

As you have these discussions, it's important that the key stakeholders are in attendance when the most important decisions are made. If they're not able to attend the entire design sprint, have them attend this day. If they can't attend the entire day, have them present when you converge on the storyboard and wireframes. Ask that they not duck out for emails, calls, or meetings during these sessions. This way, they'll be part of the decisions. If they need to change anything for business reasons, they can provide that information right away while there's still time to make adjustments before the end of the design sprint, so they'll be less likely to require changes afterward.

Scrutinize Your Work

Today you'll seek to select, integrate, and expand your best ideas, and to do so you'll need them fresh in your mind. You'll start with a review of the problem you're solving, who you're solving it for, and the most important artifacts you've created.

You'll begin this like you did when starting the Diverge phase, by going over your materials for the background phase again: facts and assumptions, questions, problem statement, personas, and the user journey map. You can do that quicker this time.

Then you'll look over and reengage with the slew of materials you generated in the Diverge phase.

Then, once you've reviewed all your work, it's now time to pick it apart so you can assemble the best parts back together. Much of this work will happen with a larger group.

Including all the voices in the room will give you the best possible insights from your team. Designers, developers, executives, customer service, and marketing folks will all bring different perspectives and solutions. Keep the conversation inclusive and open.

While you're making sure you let everyone get a chance to speak, don't design by committee. As such, respectfully acknowledge the perspective of each person who speaks, but don't be afraid to disagree completely and say so. Don't be too nice.

Encourage people to "take the boxing gloves off" and argue with one another. As Jake Knapp from Google Ventures says in his blog post about Day 3 of a design sprint, "You don't want design by committee. If there's a good argument going, don't try to find middle ground or make people agree. Help the team place a bet on one of the opposing solutions and keep the other in your back pocket if it fails." He mentions that you can call on the key decision maker to weigh in and make the decision if people don't agree.

We mentioned Alex Britez from MacMillan in Chapter 3, and he stressed the importance of getting stakeholder buy-in at this stage, so he brought it to others from around his company to offer feedback during the Converge phase. "..We invited another group of stakeholders to help with discussing the next iteration of the ideas. This included some technical and research folks. With their help, we decided what pieces of each idea we wanted to test, and how we should prioritize them."

The Converge phase is key for aligning stakeholders to get behind the design sprint's outcomes. This feedback cycle is crucial for your design sprint success.

$100 Test/Risks

As you reengage with the wealth of materials you generated in the Diverge phase, there's too much to review all together in a group. With that in mind, you'll review them using an exercise that will get everyone looking at everything individually, engaging with it, and with some constraints to kickstart the converging process. A great way to do this is for everyone to indicate their top picks for where to invest your time, interest, and effort.

We'll do this by giving everyone $100 worth of fake money. If only building the actual product could be done for $100!

The team can then use the fake money to "invest" in their top picks like the super vote from the Diverge phase, but this time you'll be voting on everything that was created in all the rounds: all the storyboards and wireframes, even the 8-Ups!

Also like the super vote, you can choose to give perhaps an extra $50 worth of the fake money to key decision makers should that be needed. We don't want to give out too much of this extra fake money, or the non-decision makers might shut down and not offer up their input if their votes don't count enough.

While you're reviewing all your ideas to identify the best, it can also be a good time to flag ideas that might have associated risk. Alex Britez, Director of Digital Innovation at Macmillan Education, describes how he did this:

"We armed each participant with some colored dots, red meaning risk, and the others [of a different color] meaning value. The idea for this was to quickly identify any risks that the original group might have not considered. Everyone also had access to Post-its to write some feedback. The general rule was if your feedback is not on a Post-it, it does not exist."

Sometimes we've done a similar risks exercise simultaneously with our votes, and sometimes we haven't. As always, the design sprint process is flexible and there's a diverse set of possibilities for the exercises you can use whenever it makes sense. Do whatever will work best for you and your team.

How

1. Distribute small Post-its to the team. Make sure these look very different from the dots you used before—at least a different color.

2. Stress the nature of not voting by popularity and to be independent with votes.

3. Have everyone walk around the room, review all the ideas, and place Post-its as bets on the ideas they consider important. On these Post-its, write the amount of money you're investing in that idea.

4. Make sure the total you've invested equals $100 or the agreed upon amount. Don't cheat!

5. You can invest more than $10 on a given idea. The entire $100 might be a bit much, but $30–$40 is common.

6. Optionally, also distribute red dots or Post-its, and have the team place those on ideas they consider risky. They can write more detail about the risk on another Post-it.

7. Walk around the room individually and see what people consider important.

Difficulty: Easy

Size: Individually

Materials: All the materials from the Diverge phase, and dots or small Post-it notes

Approximate time: 10–15 minutes

Credit: Evolved from dot voting. The origins of dot voting are unclear. Professional facilitators have been using it since the 1980s.

Identify Alternatives

Throughout the Diverge phase there should have been times when there were multiple solutions for the same problem. These show up where there are two or more storyboards that show designs solving for the same job-to-be-done but in different ways. This means you actually diverged. Hooray! Now we have to resolve these different alternatives to determine which to proceed with.

The places you'll need to converge most are the places where your ideas differ. For example, square 2 of storyboard A and square 3 of storyboard B might show two ways to accomplish the same job-to-be-done. You might choose one or the other. Or perhaps you'll take elements of each of those storyboards and combine them into a new storyboard. Either way, some aspects will be edited out and voilà, you'll have converged.

If two conflicting alternatives both seem promising, instead of choosing one or the other, you could find a way to test both. Be careful, as this will increase your scope, but you may be surprised at which one resonates more with users. This difference gives you the opportunity to consider ideas that might have otherwise been overlooked as you ran with a single path. Different or conflicting approaches are helpful because they illuminate possible choices for your product.

How

1. Affix the user journey map up on the wall, white-board, or giant easel-sized Post-it. If the user journey map has too many Post-its stuck to it already, take a photo of it and remove the Post-its, or re-draw a clean version of the user journey map.

2. Have people remove Post-its from anyone's individual storyboards and wireframes, and stick them next to the relevant part of the user journey. Take a picture of the storyboard first so you've preserved the drawing next to the written details.

3. Place different solutions to the same problem next to each other so you can see them together at the same time for ease of comparison.

4. Alternatively, people can write the idea down in a couple words on a new Post-it and attach that to the relevant area of the user journey map.

5. As a group, review the alternatives you've posted, and discuss the relative merits of each alternative.

6. Brainstorm and discuss any other important conflicting alternatives that hadn't been posted yet. Write those up too as you discuss them.

Difficulty: Moderate

Size: Individually, then as a group

Materials: The user journey map, Post-its

Approximate time: 30–60 minutes

Don't go down a "rathole" by narrowing yourself into too small an area without considering what happens before and after.

Credit: Andrew Cohen, Corwin Harrell, Trace Wax from thoughtbot, and C. Todd Lombardo from Constant Contact

2x2 Matrix (optional)

Sometimes dot voting doesn't contextualize the implementation of the possible solutions and the matrix will help define the ideas relative to one another in the context of particular criteria.

A good way to do that is to categorize alternative solutions according to criteria that will tease out their relative value. This can lead you to the solutions most likely to validate or invalidate your hypotheses.

How

1. Draw a Cartesian coordinate "+" on a board.
2. Define your x and y axes: these could be "value to user" or "cost of implementation."
3. Place all of the solutions on the matrix based on where the solution would fall.
4. The teams will discuss and debate where exactly each should fall. Having a cross-functional representation in the room will help the process. It may not go smoothly, but you'll have greater alignment.
5. Select the quadrant that encompasses the desired traits.
6. Should there still be too many solutions to pursue, consider repeating this process with another matrix and change at least one of the axes.

Difficulty: Difficult

Size: Team

Materials: Small Post-its and a wall or whiteboard to draw the axes

Don't place the items on top of each other (you need to be able to read them).

Approximate time: 15–45 minutes

Credit: The 2x2 Matrix was first used by Boston Consulting Group as the "Boston Matrix" or growth share matrix. It has evolved to many variants since.

ASSUMPTION	TEST WITH	SUCCESS CRITERIA

ASSUMPTION ✓✓

CUSTOMERS WANT TO
INTERACT W/ DATA 50 — A/B MAP v FORM

CUST. USE DATA ✓ 30
OR DIRECT MARKETING — WEB ANALYTICS

CUSTOMERS WILL
PAY TO INTERACT
W/ DATA

SMALL BIZ ONLY → PAST CMRS | MOCKUP OR FLOW/APP →

CORE FEATURES —
MORE USE 25 → MOCKUP →

MORE FLEX SEARCH... OFFER MAILED
TARGETING IS IMPT!

WE KNOW THE PROCESS 70 ~ ?
FOR CREATING A CAMPAIGN MOCKUP →
IN... (SEQUENCE)

NOT NAT'L = NO BIG PLAYERS

GEOGRAPHY
IS ALWAYS IN MIND   SURVEY

THERE IS VALUE IN RFP
UNHAPPY W/ LISTS   65 ✓✓   CMR INTERVIEWS
BUYING 'GOOD' LISTS
IS DIFFICULT

TEST WITH

A/B MAP v FORM

WEB ANALYTICS

SUCCESS CRITERIA

CONVERSION ...→ PAGES

RANKED IN TOP 3

CMRS PURCHASE
MULTIPLE LISTS

PAYMENT CADENCE   BIZ MODEL
= MONTHLY ?   260 (?) PAY FLOW TEST
PRESCRIPTIVE VS PREDICTIVE

10 15 25
20 10
25
50 20
10 30

50
50 10

Review Assumptions

You've now sorted through the ideas and some of the best ones have risen to the top, but there still will be too many to pursue. Some of them will be obvious and won't have much risk, but others imply underlying risky assumptions. These will be where you get the most benefit from testing.

When you get to your converged wireframe, your prototype, and your test plan, you'll want to get the highest risk assumptions out of the way first. If you have the time and talent to prototype and validate everything you came up with, go right ahead. The reality is you won't be able to create a prototype to validate all your assumptions.

Why prioritize your assumptions? Because you'll likely have a ton of them and won't be able to validate every single one. And if you don't have too many, you haven't yet pushed your brain to come up with the full list. You'll need to prioritize them according to confidence and risk. How confident are you they are true and how risky are they?

How

1. On a large whiteboard, start with your list of assumptions from the Facts and Assumptions exercise from the first day.

2. To the right of each assumption, add columns for "test with" and "success criteria."

3. Have each person take five minutes to generate any additional assumptions that are not already listed, and write them on Post-its.

4. Add those assumptions to the board. You can brainstorm a few others as a group if you wish.

5. Fill in the "Test With" and "Success Criteria" fields. For "Test With," many of those will be just "prototype" but other things could be "survey," "interviews," or things like "A/B tests" that will take place outside the scope of the sprint.

6. Prioritize them with the $100 test described earlier. If there are too many assumptions, you can prioritize them before filling in how you'll test them and what the success criteria would be.

Difficulty: Moderate

Size: Individually, then as a group

Materials: Assumptions from the Facts and Assumptions exercise, a large whiteboard, ability to admit what you don't know

Approximate time: 30–45 minutes

Don't think you have all the assumptions identified.

Credit: Trevor Owens from Javelin Software, based on Eric Ries' Lean Startup methodology, adding in inspiration from Craig Launcher from Assumption Storming

Wireframe the Prototype

This is where it all comes together. You've got your assumptions prioritized. You've got your user story. You've got your jobs-to-be-done. You've even got a set of the storyboard frames that seem the most promising ones this side of the Mississippi has ever seen.

Now it's time to assemble them into the storyboard of wireframes that show how the user will interact with your prototype, click by click, tap by tap, or swipe by swipe.

At this point, there are usually still just a few too many storyboard frames and screens to know which to use. You're in the home stretch for narrowing them down, and this is where the rubber meets the road and you can make some hard decisions. You'll converge your ideas first in teams, then with the whole group.

Team Sketching

With the best concepts fresh in your mind, you now need to organize them. You've done that mostly individually thus far, and you're at a point where you can converge into proposed user interactions that can pass the scrutiny of the group.

You'll divide into teams, and each team will choose one person as a scribe. But this isn't just their show. The group will be discussing each frame as you go along, and the scribe will put large pen to large paper to reflect that input, based on all the sketches that came before.

This works best in bursts of about 30 minutes. You don't want the scope to be too large, so as before, divide the user journey map into at least two chunks. Each of these will get a team sketch. There may be parts of the user journey map that aren't in the scope of what you want to prototype and test. If so, leave those parts aside.

Know that each sketch will get strong critiques in the ritual dissent to follow, but don't worry about that yet. You'll also criticize others' ideas in kind, and that's part of the deal. Confidently put your best ideas out there, and trust that the process will take care of surfacing the right ideas that will get to move forward.

There usually isn't time to do multiple cycles of team sketching on the same part of the user journey map, so have one team focus on one part and another team focus on the other part. That way, the other team(s) can incorporate the feedback.

As always with these converging exercises, be very frank and vocal with your comments. Expect a good amount of debate as your drawings come together.

How

1. Divide into two teams. If any team has more than three or four people, divide into more teams.

2. Divide the user journey map into two or more parts. Give a different part to each team. Note that you'll need a team sketching/ritual dissent cycle for each of these sections of the user journey map.

3. Set a timer for 30 minutes.

4. Have each team choose a scribe.

5. On large 25" × 30" easel-sized Post-its, have each group create a hybrid storyboard/wireframe to illustrate the user's interaction with their part of the user journey map. This can still include human-human interaction in storyboard frames, but mostly will be wireframes for how users will interact with your product.

6. Even though only one team member is drawing, make sure each team member contributes. If someone isn't talking much, give them the pen and ask them to draw!

7. Keep your sketch moving at a good clip, so you don't run out of time.

Pro Tip: If you think you'll want to change your sketch (and you will want to change your sketch!) draw in pencil first with an eraser handy, then spend the last couple minutes tracing over it with a Sharpie. Or instead, you could represent each frame on large Post-its stuck to the sheet from the large easel pad.

Difficulty: Easy
Size: Individually
Materials: All the materials from the Diverge phase, and dots or small Post-it notes

Approximate time: 30 minutes

Don't lose track of time. Don't let anyone dominate the conversation about what gets drawn.

Credit: Evolved from Will Evans' Design Studio methodology[2] and the 3-12-3 exercise from *Gamestorming*[3] as adapted by Kyle Fiedler, Chief Design Officer at thoughtbot

---

2 Will Evans, "Introduction to Design Studio Methodology," August 5, 2014, *http://www.uie.com/articles/design_studio_methodology*.

3 Dave Gray, "3-12-3 Brainstorm," October 27, 2010, *http://bit.ly/3-12-3-storm*.

Ritual Dissent

You've got your first group sketches suggesting how your product can address the needs of your users, now it's time to tear them apart. Some of these solutions will be solid, but others might have gaps, holes, and reasons they might not work. Another team will also be proposing a solution, so you'll need to criticize each other so the best ideas bubble to the top.

In a ritual dissent, each group chooses a spokesperson to present their idea. After presenting it, the spokesperson should turn around and face the wall. That way, people won't be looking directly at the presenter while they give their critiques. That will help them be more honest as the presenter won't be looking them in the eye for approval.

The goal of this exercise is to shoot as many holes in ideas as possible, to see which solutions can survive these attacks. So this is the time where the gloves really come off. There's only a 5-minute window to give this feedback, so it will be especially blunt. The exercise won't work if people soften or temper their feedback so it may come off as harsh, but don't take it personally.

You'll have time for two ritual dissent sessions. If you have two groups, do the ritual dissent with the entire group. If you have more than two groups, do the ritual dissent in smaller groups.

How

1. Select a spokesperson for each group.

2. If you have two groups, have each spokesperson present to everyone there. If you have more than two groups, have each spokesperson bring their drawing to another group, and the ritual dissents can happen in parallel.

3. Set a timer for 5 minutes. In that time, the spokesperson presents the wireframe/storyboard as if it was being presented to a group of investors.

4. The group listens in silence and takes notes as they think of problems with the idea.

5. The spokesperson faces the wall, away from those critiquing. If she's presenting to the entire room, her group should turn around as well.

6. The team members offers their critiques, candidly attacking everything wrong with the idea. They should be as direct as possible. Don't hold back.

7. The spokesperson (and her group) listens in silence and takes notes. In this exercise, they can't respond to comments or defend their ideas.

Difficulty: Moderate

Size: Entire group if there are two groups in the team sketches, or subgroups if there were more than two

Materials: For presenters, drawings, pen and paper to take notes, an open mind, and a thick skin; for everyone else, bring your harshest criticism and your most outgoing mood

Approximate time: 20 minutes

Credit: Will Evans and Jacklyn Burgan[4]

---

4 Jacklyn Burgan, "Intro to Agile and Lean UX," October 23, 2013, http://www.slideshare.net/jacklynburgan/intro-leanux-turnerfinal.

Repeat the Converge Cycle

If you broke the user journey map into more than two parts, you'll need multiple cycles. Repeat the team sketch and ritual dissent exercises as described earlier.

You'll be going over the same ground that another group presented and that you then criticized. As such, you can now address the problems raised by your own critiques. For each part of your drawing, you want to propose the best solution possible. If the previous solution was the most solid one presented, you don't need to change it, but you also don't have to keep it the same. Whenever you can think of a better solution, go with that!

These choices aren't final. You'll have an opportunity to pick the best options in your final group wireframe, and you can also expect things to change a lot after you receive user feedback and proceed beyond the design sprint.

Final Sketch

With just a few options bubbling to the top, you've now converged enough to create your final wireframe. This will be similar to the group sketches you just did, but with the entire group present this time.

As before, choose a scribe with good drawing skills. And as before, it's not just up to them. The whole group needs to contribute, and the person with the pen is just the one who's writing it all down.

This will take a lot of room, so if you don't have two whiteboards or walls with a lot of IdeaPaint and open space, you might do better with big easel-sized 25" × 30" Post-its. Use as many as you need.

This ends up looking like a giant comic book drawing, with a whole bunch of little frames, starring your product and users as the superheroes. Keep your user journey map handy so you can tell the entire story, or at least the part of it you know you want to prototype and test.

You'll go frame by frame, screen by screen, drawing heavily from the group sketches you just did, and also from the best sketches and ideas from the rest of the sprint. If you can't decide between multiple options, feel free to ask the user experience designer or the main stakeholder.

How

1. Draw a big grid on the whiteboard or on several easel-sized Post-its (each frame should be about the size of two sheets of paper).
2. For each frame, discuss and draw a single screen of the user interacting with your product. Refer to your previous group and individual sketches. Ensure everyone speaks up.
3. Keep drawing frames until you've covered the parts of the user journey map that you've chosen to prototype and test.
4. If you notice that the scope is too large, feel free to hone in just on the most important areas to test.

Difficulty: Difficult
Size: Entire group
Materials: Multiple whiteboards (or easel-sized Post-its)

Approximate time: 1–2 hours

Don't sit in silence without giving feedback while the scribe draws the entire wireframe alone.

Credit: Wireframing with a group has been popular for a while. Jake Knapp at Google Ventures documented the process in his blog posts about the product design sprint.

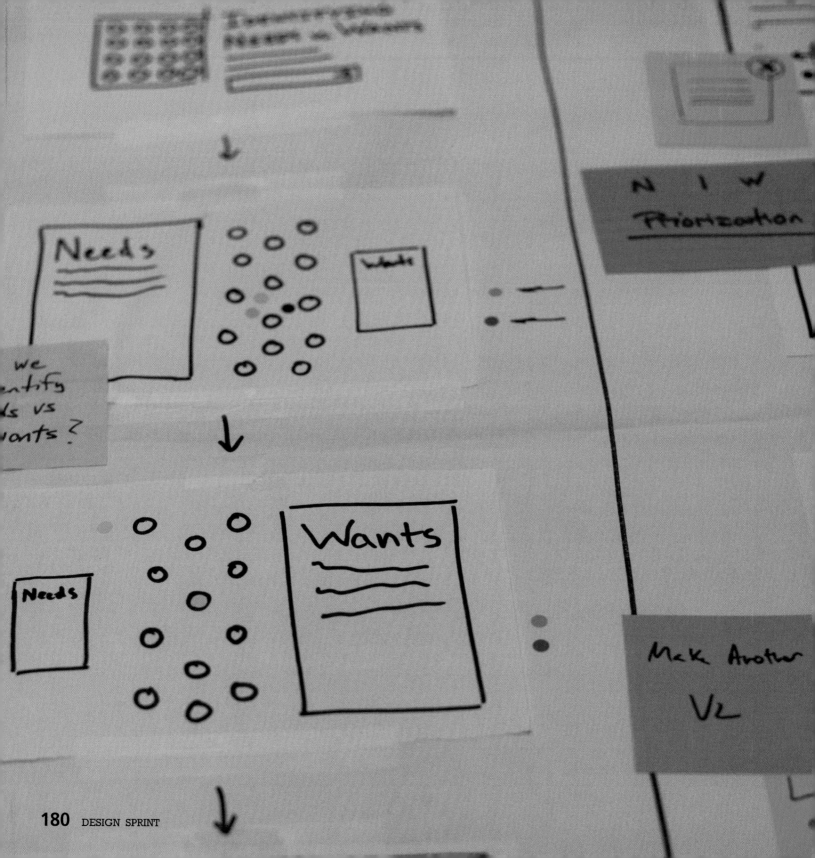

Takeaways:

- There won't be time to test all ideas, so you'll need to prioritize and choose.

- Lay out a storyboard for the interaction you decide on, and convert that into wireframes.

- Ensure shy people have their say.

- Ensure key stakeholders are present.

- There are several fun and proven ways to include all team members. Use these methods to get the best results.

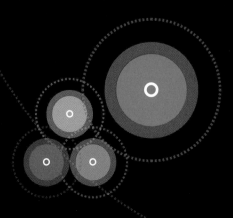

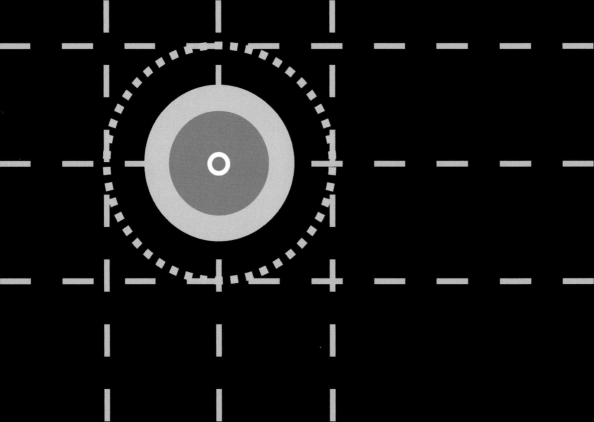

Phase 4: Prototype

You're almost ready, and you have narrowed down what you need to build. During this phase you will build a prototype—it could be quick-and-dirty, low fidelity, or high fidelity. All product prototypes are living versions of the idea you have in your head. These tangible prototypes need not be perfect but should provide enough detail to be able to test adequately the assumptions your team has made. The goal here is not perfection. Don't get stuck in endless loops trying to make your prototype look like the final product. That won't help you. The goal here is to create a mockup your users can interact with—something that can test your hypothesis and validate or invalidate your assumptions. Because you typically have only one day to build the prototype, it should be as high fidelity as needed, and nothing more.

What Happens During the Prototype Phase?

Schedule and/or Confirm Interviews	~1 hour
Build the Prototype	~6 hours
Finalize the Test Plan	~30 minutes

Recommended Agenda

You need an agenda? Just go make it!

Schedule and/or Confirm the Interviews

Check Your Users Against the Target Persona

If you have already scheduled appointments with test subjects, you are ahead of the game. If those people match the personas you've identified, even better! If neither of those are true, it's time to scramble. While the designers and/or developers are making the prototype, other participants spend the day recruiting and scheduling the tests.

Recruiting Test Takers: Where to Find People?

Depending on your persona(s), there could be a variety of means to find users. If you're in a large city and your persona is a consumer, you may be able to recruit some via a Craigslist ad, or even by approaching people on the street. However, like Laura Klein, author of *Lean UX for Startups*, we also discourage approaching random people in a coffee shop.[1] First, it's just plain creepy. Second, you are less likely to find your target user. Remember all that thought you put into the personas and journey on the first phase? Find someone who's about to embark on that journey, someone who needs that job-to-be-done!

Your existing user/customer base. If you have a user or customer base to draw from, this is a great place to start. Internal sales and marketing teams can often point you in the right direction to connect with the subset of existing customers. At Constant Contact, the Innovation team has built something called "Test Drive," a network

---

1 *http://bit.ly/klein-coffee*

of more than 7,000 Constant Contact small businesses customers that have opted in to test and provide feedback on new products and services. Trace and Richard work closely with their respective clients to obtain and identify the appropriate users for testing. Further, Richard and his team have developed relationships with different organizations such as the Alzheimer's Association and The Perkins School for the Blind to source test participants when they need to test prototypes for accessibility.

Craigslist. The large classified ad platform has many communities across the globe, and we've used their "gigs" section to recruit users for a variety of tests. The warning here is to be sure you're screening appropriately with a survey, which we'll get to in a moment. There's always trepidation given the negative press Craigslist sometimes receives, so be careful and screen your test subjects. We don't want to read about your prototype attempts in the daily news, OK?

Amazon's Mechanical Turk (MTurk). This crowdsourcing network gives you access to participants from around the world who are willing to take short online "HITS" for low cost, often pennies. MTurk may not have high-quality responses, nor will you find users that fit into a narrowly defined category. Further, many users on MTurk quickly take tests and can falsely answer your questions, so be sure to include some screener questions to determine which results to keep or discard.

Panel agencies. Services such as Opinions for Good (Op4G), which focuses on non-profits, and Research Now offer lists of users you are able to filter and select according to your needs. There is often a direct cost associated with these types of agencies as that's their business model. But they can be a worthwhile investment: you'll get a higher quality response from someone who represents your user base.

Web-based services. User testing sites such as *usertesting.com*, *trymyui.com,* and *applause.com* offer captured narrative services with a population of users to select from. Because these are remote and unmoderated, you may not be able to interact directly with the users. While these can be hugely valuable at later stages of product development, they may not be best for a design sprint. You want to be able to see the user's face and body language if you can, because it can often tell you more than she is actually saying.

Your existing social networks. We've seen many requests on Facebook, LinkedIn, and Twitter calling for users to test a prototype. It's always tempting to reach out to people who you know and have an established relationship with; however, be careful, as they may not make great test participants, as they are less likely to give you the honest, critical feedback you need.

Screen Out the Users Who Don't Fit

A screener survey can help you filter out responses of users who do not fit the profile of the users you have identified (personas, FTW!). Conduct one or two short surveys that filter out the types of users you seek. Here is an example screener survey we used at Constant Contact:

1.   Do you own a small business?
2.   Does your business have a website?
3.   Does your business have a Facebook page?
4.   Do you engage in email marketing activity to promote your business and/or brand?
5.   How many email newsletters per month do you send?

These five simple questions help us to find a subset of users who are small business owners, who have a website and a Facebook page, and also participate in some frequency of email marketing activity. You'll want to check the business website and Facebook pages to verify it is not someone looking to answer a few questions for a few dollars. Speaking of dollars...

Compensation: pay them something, even if it isn't money

A technique C. Todd often uses is to not offer any particular financial compensation to schedule the interview. This reduces the likelihood of someone taking the test because they want a quick buck. When the test is over, he'll send the participant a thank-you card and a $25 gift card in the mail. This "delighter" approach is unexpected and shows the user how valuable her time was to you and the team. Other things we have seen used as compensation range from a simple cup of coffee, to lunch, to a free month of your product or service if you charge a monthly fee, and even free swag. One of the most powerful draws we have found is early access to new products, product features, or services. If you've struck the right nerve, you'll have users clamoring for access to your product as soon as possible, and this is one of the best outcomes.

Build the Prototype

- Any copy to be included (for goodness' sake, no *Lorem Ipsum,* please!)
- Your sketches, wireframes, and storyboards
- More coffee
- A maker's mindset

You may be thinking "what if I'm not a designer?!" That's OK, prototyping digital products can be done using paper, Keynote, PowerPoint, HTML, or a prototyping tool (e.g., Invision, Proto.io, Balsamiq, etc.). You don't need to be skilled in HTML/CSS or the Adobe Creative Suite to make something to test. The act of making something gives the product life beyond the concepts and allows the design to be experienced for the first time by people outside your immediate team. In the world of digital prototypes, the process of developing a prototype might be more important than the end product itself. This is very similar to writing a business plan. It's not the end product that matters; it's the mental exercise of thinking through the plan that will give you insights you need in the future.

The prototype, whether it's on paper or online, is a test vehicle that will include some content, some of the primary navigation, and possibly important copy or images as well as the key functional elements.

Who Should Be Involved

If you're doing the design sprint as an internal exercise (i.e., without the help of a design partner), then you may only need to include your initial design sprint team. However, if you are fortunate to have the help of a competent designer, you can shift some of the work to them. Alex Britez at MacMillan usually finds himself and one other colleague prototyping while the rest of the team has either returned to their "day jobs" or are helping set up the interviews. If you're running the design sprint as a design firm, then the client's core team and your core design team will be involved. Ideally you want the prototyping team to be small. Inviting more people doesn't invite better input. What was it about too many cooks?

The goal is to get something ready for the validate phase that will take place the following day. So once you have your prototype mocked up, get final feedback from your team and then agree on an endpoint, so you don't wind up going in circles. This can be difficult if there are additional approvals or sign-offs required. It's essential that you spend enough time before you start this process educating your clients, participants, and/or stakeholders that prototyping work is not to secure approval on the aesthetics or functional elements; rather, it is to define and refine the flow and navigation of the future product.

It can be very daunting, as we have seen many people conflate the prototype and test with deciding on product direction. When Marc Guy at Faze-1 arrived at this stage, the look on his face was incredibly conflicted. He initially thought that making this prototype was going to set the direction for the product. And because they were a startup at the time, this would dictate the direction his company was headed. C. Todd realized that this was going on in Marc's head and reminded him this was only a test. No need to break the glass and pull the fire alarm—it's just a test, and should be used as an opportunity to learn.

This is only a test.

Review the Previous Day's Work and Plan the Day

The day starts with reviewing the decisions you made the day before and confirming which parts of the previous day's designs will be used in the prototype(s). If you are planning on making more than one prototype, then we recommend dividing into groups and working on the designs separately. Plan to have working periods followed by rests in approximately 90-minute cycles. We also recommend you start each new design session by bringing the group together and doing a quick review or critique of the previous session (only spend 5 minutes at most for these short critiques).

Delegate and Assign Tasks

You only have one day to build your prototype, so the best approach is to spread the design work across your team. Don't worry too much about the consistency of the design elements. Use the morning to get the critical elements in place and use the afternoon to bring them all together in a consistent design pattern. Having one person to coordinate the designs across the group or groups will help tie things up at the end of the day. This work burns calories so make sure there's plenty of coffee and snacks. Additionally, other team members may be confirming or setting your interview schedule (more about this later).

Sketch First, Mock Up Later (Or Not)

You should have a clear idea of what you're building from the Converge phase. There may be some discussion on the nuances remaining and depending on how far your Converge phase went, you might have a set of sketches defined. Your prototype should include all of the elements that were "touched" by the users in the Test phase. If you're creating more than one prototype, you'll need to decide if elements are going to be used across the board or used discretely in the different prototypes.

Common elements like browser bars and fonts should be decided on before you create anything. Often we find that a company's brand and/or style guide has sufficient depth to pull this information from. If there's no brand guide? Go basic, it's not about the fonts and colors, so move forward with paper prototype with POP App if you struggle with getting something built. Remember: this is about learning—we cannot stress this enough.

Make It

At this stage, less is more—only focus on the essentials. Do not be tempted to fill in all the gaps and fill up the space on the home or landing pages you are sketching. That level of detail will come later. Drawing out the site pages helps everyone involved to visualize what you are doing. Getting everyone on the same page, literally, is critical to understanding where the design will succeed and where it needs more help. As discussed in the previous chapter, the first prototype designs happen on a whiteboard or a piece of paper and are then transferred in more detail to Keynote, Illustrator, Sketch, or other tool. If you've separated the work across different team members, you may have some inconsistency in the design. Leave time at the end of the day to clean up the designs and make them look like a single product.

Having created your core product pages or flows, you can begin to build out the complete prototype. As for public-facing sections of your product, we start with the key entry points (e.g., home page, registration page, download page) and a few primary pages. If you're designing a web application, you'll also want to design the critical functional areas (e.g., dashboard, profile setup/edit, and uploading files). Each project will be slightly different, but you'll notice patterns in all of them.

We're big fans of sketching, but in order to create a "true-to-life" design of a digital product, we recommend building your prototype in something that can be made interactive. POP is a great tool for bringing your sketches to life. Keynote and PowerPoint can be just as valuable and there are lots of kits commercially available on the market for relatively low cost. The most popular one we have seen is Keynotopia,[2] which offers file formats in both Apple Keynote and Microsoft PowerPoint. At the time of this writing, there are a number of other web-based prototyping tools available such as Marvel App, Proto.io, and Pixate, none of which require coding knowledge.

A Word of Warning

If you are planning on using sophisticated design tools like Illustrator, Sketch, or Photoshop (or even HTML/CSS code) in the Prototype phase, you risk becoming bogged down. Unless you are an experienced designer who can create the prototype in a few hours (or you have someone on your team who can), we recommend sticking with something simpler.

If you are working with a copywriter, add simple text fields, which can be updated later. We are not in favor of using *lorem ipsum* to fill in blank spaces. No *hipster ipsum* nor *cupcake ipsum* either, though C. Todd might be swayed if *cookie ipsum* was a thing. Lack of clear content is an indication you are unsure what the value proposition is, and it creates administrative debris to clean up later. In testing, you don't want to hear things like, "What does this mean?" It distracts from the goal of your prototype: to learn about your assumptions. So use real words and if necessary have your content strategist or copywriter update it either in parallel, or after you are done building your prototype.

---

2 *http://keynotopia.com/*

In the design firm setting, to achieve the speed of execution our clients expect, we move directly from prototypes to validation and then once we have feedback we move to low-fidelity mockups. The client reviews these mockups and any changes required are made immediately. Because we publish the designs to the Web via Basecamp, we find progress is only limited by the speed at which we can get feedback. In some cases, we'll move from sketches to HTML/CSS immediately so we can make updates even faster. This can only be achieved if you have sign off on a design flow or concept.

Prototyping Tools

You'll want to select the simplest, fastest tool that can best validate your assumptions. We recommend any of the following to create your prototype:

- Paper prototypes
- Keynotopia/PowerPoint
- Storyboards
- Physical objects
- Web-based prototyping tools (e.g., POP, InVision, proto.io, Marvel App, Flinto, and Pixate)
- HTML/CSS

Examples of Prototypes

Project: Great Engagements

Summary: Before couples can address the details of planning a wedding (decoration, guests, caterers, dress, etc.), couples usually have to decide on a location and venue. The couple is filled with excitement, as the wedding day will usher forth a new life for the couple together. However, the couple might experience a bit of uncertainty as to how even to proceed planning their wedding. We want to capture couples at their "excitement" period and put aside all uncertainty and potential anxiety that the wedding planning process may cause. A customer's initial engagement with our website should parallel his/her engagement with the wedding process in general.

Prototype: An interactive website (see image)

Learning: With this prototype, the team wanted to learn how well their website captured the excitement of a recently engaged couple.

Project: SMB Marketing Smarts

Summary: Due to a trending increase in mobile device usage and web page analytics showing a greater percentage of hits to its support forums and help articles from mobile devices, Constant Contact was interested in creating an easy-to-navigate mobile app that packaged its wealth of educational resources and included the ability to push a button and connect via phone to the customer support center.

Prototype: An interactive mobile app created with Proto.io (see images). In total, eight different screens were created with interaction hot spots.

Learning: With this prototype, the team wanted to learn if and how Constant Contact users would interact with a mobile app to get help for marketing-related questions.

Finalize the Test Plan

As part of the team is preparing the prototype, others can work on structuring the test interview. We strongly recommend in-person interviews when possible, but we have been in situations where that's just not possible. It's not like these users can easily make their way to your office, and depending on your geography, it may be a challenge to get to the right users. In such situations, we rely on a virtual setup using a variety of tools we'll discuss later. Now is the perfect time to review your assumptions and consider your hypotheses for testing.

Assumptions Table/Validation Board

We mentioned previously that the design sprint is like a mini science experiment. What's done here is to have another look at the assumptions table. Are there any assumptions missing? At Constant Contact, we use a validation board at this stage to determine what you may test at the end of the design sprint. You will not complete the entire board, because you have no test results yet, but you should have a clear idea of what needs to be tested. Prioritize your assumptions and determine which your prototype will test.

How

Work with key stakeholders in initial sponsor meeting to complete the core hypothesis and success criteria components of the validation board. This can be completed before the sprint or during the Understand phase. It doesn't have to be perfect at first, but by the time you're prototyping it should be quite solidified.

1. Craft your hypothesis.
2. List all your relevant assumptions (best practice is to list them in order of importance with your lynchpin assumption at the top).
3. Define your success criteria.
4. State what you will you measure along the way.
5. Describe the actual test.

6. Once the test is complete, examine data and see if your core hypothesis is still true or if it was invalidated? Move [copy] your assumptions into validate or invalidated boxes and summarize with your conclusions and recommendations.

Difficulty: Moderate

Size: Individual or teams

Materials: Blank validation board

Context: Good to start before or at the beginning of the sprint and by the end have a full outline of the work completed.

Approximate time: 15–20 minutes to start (more time can be allotted depending on the size and nature of the experiment)

Credit: Trevor Owens of Javelin Software created the first validation board for idea validation. There have been many variants since.

Decide on the Pre-Roll Questions

We use the term "pre-roll" to mean any questions you ask before getting the user interacting with the prototype. These questions establish the context and surface information regarding their behaviors, attitudes, and beliefs. It's similar to a contextual inquiry, but on a smaller scale. You'll build rapport with the person you're interviewing because… they are a human! We're not saying this to be condescending—we have been guilty ourselves of being a little too robotic on test day. Humans are complex, so establishing a good relationship at the beginning will help you learn what you need.

Example "pre-roll" questions that went along with the SMB Marketing Smarts example shown earlier:

1. How do you find content for your email newsletters?
2. At what stage do you find you have unanswered questions?
3. What steps do you take to answer those questions?
4. How long does it take you to find an answer?

Define the Tasks

When testing your prototype, you want to see how the user will navigate to accomplish particular tasks. While this may not be 100% like a textbook usability test, there needs to be a starting point, or a reason for the user to interact with your prototype. What specifically would a user do? Consider the job stories you worked on earlier in the week.

Example tasks for SMB Marketing Smarts prototype:

Task #1: You're just about to send your next newsletter. How would you find ideas for the newsletter content?

Task #2: You just sent your monthly newsletter and now need to share it on social media. How would you accomplish that?

Create the Post-Roll Questions

Once the user has completed the test of your prototype, you'll want to ask a handful of questions to wrap up the session. These questions should help you to understand how easy or difficult it was for users to accomplish the tasks you asked them to complete. We always recommend two concluding questions: one to gauge the necessity of the prototype in the users' lives and the second to determine what the most pressing things are in their worlds at the moment.

1. How difficult was it to accomplish Task 1? ... 2? ... 3?
2. On a scale of 1 to 10, with 1 being "Yawn" and 10 being "I need this yesterday," where does this product fall?
3. What is the one thing that could be fixed tomorrow in your business? What type of product would be something "you need yesterday"?

With the prototype made, and interviews scheduled and structured, you're now ready to put rubber to the road!

Takeaways

- Schedule and find users from your existing user base, through clients and through places such as Craigslist, MTurk, and professional panels such as UserTesting.com.

- Use real human language and avoid typos. Overly complicated language can intimidate or frustrate a user and cause them to become anxious.

- Focus the creation of the prototype on the testing of major assumptions, like the value proposition and the primary user experience. Don't get caught up in the details. What colors and design elements to use are less important to your testing than knowing if your users understand what problem you're trying to solve for them.

- Finalize your test plan to have pre-roll, task test, and post-roll questions.

- Use the simplest tool that can most effectively validate your assumptions. Do not try to be fancy. This is not the time to be a prima donna. You seek to learn, not impress.

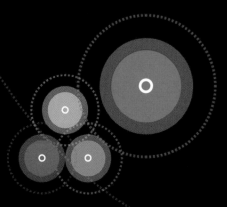

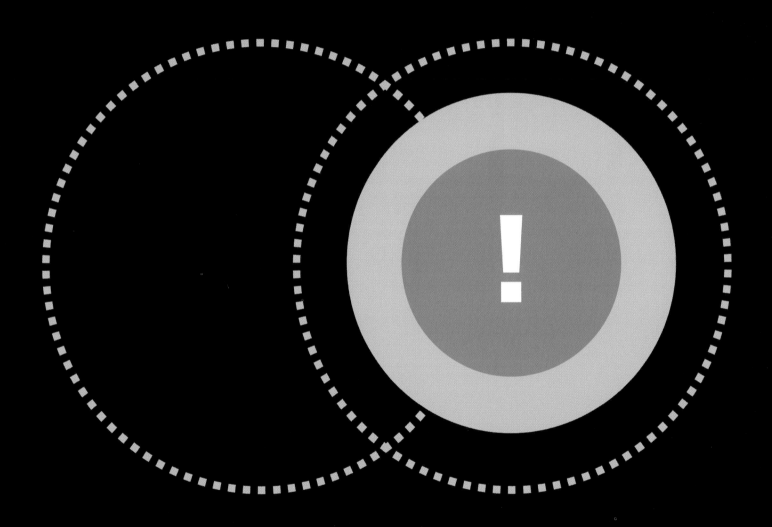

Chapter 9

Phase 5: Test

Rubber, meet road. Are you ready? Your users (or customers) are the ones who will give you the best feedback possible. This is where you get to see their pupils dilate, their smiles widen, and voices rise in reaction to your prototype. It is also when you can be greatly disappointed. If you consider your personal journey map along your design sprint, this is the point where your emotions run high, as you have spent a lot of energy up to this point and you're hoping that everything will work. Be prepared if things go wrong. Sometimes they don't, yet most times they do. It's OK—to our knowledge, no humans were ever harmed by a design sprint.

What Happens During the Test Phase?

Test Your Prototype: Up to 6 hours

Debrief and Retrospective: Up to 1 hour

Recommended Agenda

Nike says "Just do it." We say "Just test it!" Here's what this day often looks like:

9:00	**Interview #1**
10:00	**Interview #2**
11:00	**Interview #3**
12:00	**Quick Lunch**
	Have a good-natured (read: snarky) conversation about what went wrong during the first three interviews. Make tweaks to fix the simple things.
1:00	**Interview #4**
2:00	**Interview #5**
	Twiddle thumbs and quietly mutter curses when user doesn't show up. Find a remote user to speak to in their place.
3:00	**Interview #6**
4:00	**Debrief and Discuss Next Steps**
	End with final recap/retrospective.

Test Your Prototype

The goal of the Test phase is not just to confirm that the product you have prototyped is good, but that it's the right prototype. There's no point in doing all this work if you can't validate that this product would have a positive impact on the lives of the people who would use it and that it's relevant to your businesses' larger goals.

Keep the user testing simple by restricting it to a handful of target customers. For most product teams, it's realistic to get five to seven people to test the product. We've seen as many as 15 tested in a single day. This is probably the upper limit of what can be squeezed into one day and still obtain quality feedback. Larger sample sizes are not necessarily better. Although statistically less important, once you reach seven or eight people, you typically start hearing repetitive information and the likelihood of learning something new is diminished.

We don't recommend using groups to test your product. Focus groups have their place, however they are not the most effective method to test product flow and features, because they amplify biases and individual opinions. This group testing approach has been popular in consumer products for decades and it's a recipe for bad results for digital products. We've often observed situations in which a test user with a strong personality unwittingly influences other members of the focus group. In these group scenarios, the testers will be swayed, or even emotionally bullied, by the other people in the group, and you don't want that. "Groupthink" is avoidable simply by testing the participants separately.

Tools for Testing

The tools you use will depend on the type of prototype you've created. As you're creating digital products in the design sprint, you may need the digital devices you've designed for. If your prototype is a mocked-up version of a mobile app, you'll need the mobile app that people would use it on. This setup normally required two locations, one for the test customer and one for the observers. In our experience these are not always going to be rooms. It's very possible that you might have a test subject being tested on the street and the observers sitting back at the office. You'll have one observer with the test customer, and the rest of the team will be observing from afar. It's our advice that you shouldn't have more than one tester in the room with the participant. It can be intimidating for certain personality types.

The Testing Environment

To test successfully, you'll need to have the person being interviewed, your test subject, a device of some sort, and the observers hooked up to a screen-sharing and video-sharing product so you can watch the action. If you're not good at audio/visual setups, you might need a little help with this part.

At a minimum, we recommend the following things:

- A few consent forms
- Notebooks and pens
- A camera with video capabilities
- A tripod for the camera (optional)
- A separate recording device (this is optional, but we like to grab the audio and send it to a transcription service so we have a written record of each interview; it's easier to scan these notes rather than rewatch an entire video)

- Apple Airplay, Skype, GoToMeeting, Google Hangouts, Zoom, or any video-conferencing application that has screen-sharing capabilities
- If necessary, a set of speakers or a speaker phone for the observation audience to listen into the testing audio (assuming your video conferencing service needs this addition)
- Test goals, questions, and tasks written out for the tester to ask the participant during the test
- Whiteboard to track assumptions and testing goals (you'll want to list all your testing goals here and track them against your test subject responses or feedback)

A Word of Warning: Don't leave setup until the last minute. A/V setups can be cruel and malfunctioning, even in this day and age. Someone in your office is a total nerd—find him or her and ask for help. Test the setup before your first test is scheduled.

Here's a story from the trenches: At Constant Contact, there is a Software Engineering Development Program that rotates newly graduated engineers to different engineering teams across the organization over one year's time. In their final rotation, they participated in a design sprint. On the test day, they thought they were ready to go. C. Todd asked them, "who have you tested your test setup with?" They looked at him with a slightly dumbfounded look and replied "um, no one." He then suggested testing a nearby team member before bringing in real users, so that they could ensure their setup, questions, and tasks were all in proper working order. This helped, as the team found two flaws in the test questions and eliminated a technical glitch of getting users on board with the A/V setup. It may seem meta to test the test setup, but learn from our past mistakes; it's not fun when something fails during the test.

When Possible: Go to the Users

We're big fans of getting out of the building and testing in the context of the testers' lives. If you're testing an app that is designed for use in a restaurant or at a bus stop, then try meeting your testers in those locations. This might require some extra work, but it's well worth the effort, as context is king in the real world. We've gone as far as to ride along with people on their way to catching a plane in order to test a solution we were designing for an airport client.

If you can't get out of the building and meet your test subjects in the ideal situation, then you can set up an observation room. This has advantages and disadvantages. For one, it's really simple to set up, and it's easier to capture the feedback. The observation room will be the location for your test customer, and you'll link their progress through the product to another machine in another room. This other room can be located anywhere you'd like, as you will use screen-sharing and video technology like Skype, GoToMeeting, JoinMe, or Google Hangouts to conduct the tests. If you're doing this work in a large office, you'll need to reserve two rooms. We've also used Apple Airplay and Zoom to conduct interviews. Zoom is particularly useful for testing on mobile projects because you can watch the screen of the person being tested and activate the camera to watch their expressions. At the end of the day, the simplest solution to the testing environment is very often the best solution.

It Happens: Someone Will Cancel

This happens in a majority of design sprints. Some of the scheduled users won't show up. They might have a different time zone marked on their calendar, or might have something higher priority in their schedule that morning. It's OK. By confirming the day before, users are less likely to forget. We schedule seven or eight interviews, with the expectation that a couple of the users will cancel. That way we still have feedback from five or six users.

Don't Coach Your Testers Through the Prototype

As tempting as it might be, don't walk users through the entire product step by step. Once you've told them what you want them to do (e.g., sign up for a new service, select a movie, order takeout, etc.), let them navigate through the product on their own. Observe their paths and notice where they get hung up or stuck. If they look confused, you can ask subtle questions like, "You seem stuck, are you?" or "What do you think you would do next?" If their answers don't provide enough information about what they're thinking, you can say "Talk more about that." The goal here is to observe and take notes, not to be a tour guide.

You'll also want to let the participant know it's about the content of the test and not about them personally. Make them feel comfortable in sharing their thoughts and feelings (e.g., "We're here to test the product, not to test you"). Resist answering questions about the product or business until after the interview or turn these back into questions (e.g., "Does this feature allow uploading photos directly from my phone?" can be answered with "Do you think it should allow that?").

Observing nonverbal cues is just as informative. Look for changes in facial expressions, mood, or body language. Testers might feel embarrassed if they can't figure something out, and instead of blaming the design might blame themselves. This nuanced behavior generally doesn't manifest verbally, so look for clues like frowning or fidgeting. A persons' feet can actually say a lot about their emotional state.[1]

After showing the prototype, ask each participant a question or two to gauge their excitement about using what the prototype could one day become. A variant of the growth question popularized by Sean Ellis is a good way to do this. At thoughtbot, we

---

1 Joe Navarro, "What the Feet and Legs Say About Us," November 4, 2009, *http://bit.ly/feet-legs.*

sometimes phrase the question like, "On a scale from 0–10, how disappointed would you be if you could no longer use what you just experienced?" Just keep in mind that some participants might hesitate in providing negative feedback, as they're worried about hurting your feelings. Make sure you let them know that negative feedback will be useful to help find the parts of the product that need to be removed or improved.

Note that the answer to this question may not be what you want to hear. Design sprints were created to maximize the chances of building something people want, so be prepared if the answer isn't the resounding "yes" you were hoping for. Be prepared for negative feedback, and prepare your team for receiving bad news about their favorite features. Not everything will survive the test.

Capture Artifacts

In our own testing routines, we often include a project manager (PM) to gather all the artifacts related to the interviews. This might be audio, photos, videos, screen grabs, or off-the-cuff observations made by the team. We generally organize the captured data by interviewee, but we've also seen it done by feature, question, or flow and further categorized by version if you're testing more than one prototype design. One clever technique that Alex Britez from MacMillan uses is to have the audio of the tests transcribed, which allows the team to filter out common language words (e.g., "the," "and," "so," "is," etc.) and look for other wordcount patterns.

User Test Interview

To validate or invalidate your prototype, you'll need to get it in front of the people who would actually use it. You're seeking their honest, unfiltered reactions, so keep an open mind and bring your curiosity. Ask "why" often!

How

1. Create a brief description and goal of what you're looking to understand.
2. Consider some "getting to know you" icebreaker questions to build rapport with the participants. They are human, remember!
3. After introductions, move on to your pre-roll questions to learn more about the participant and her current approach to solving the problem you've identified.
4. Briefly describe the test and ask the participant to complete whatever tasks you have identified in your preparation.
5. Resist the urge to describe how the prototype works. Silence is your friend, even if it feels awkward.
6. Once complete, ask the post-roll questions.
7. Thank the participants and ask for a business card or contact information so that you can follow up with a thank-you note.

Difficulty: Difficult

Size: Best in pairs

Materials: A/V recorder, notepad and pen, camera, topic map, and whatever you use to show your prototype

Context: A validation board and a prototype should be complete.

Don't tell the participants how to work the prototype. If they can't figure it out, your design is broken. Preferably, you would assign two sprint participants per user.

Approximate time: Up to 30 minutes (can take longer)

Credit: Testing interviews have been used for many years. Just not enough! The source is unknown.

Debrief and Retrospective

There are three typical categories of a design sprint's outcome: it worked, it didn't, and somewhere in between. It should be clear which your tests fall into overall. Some users may claim it works, while others may be completely confused. The caution here is to not cherry-pick the results to confirm what you already believe. Confirmation bias is prevalent and testing is not always a hardline black-or-white answer, which is why we call out our assumptions in prior activities.

When It Works as Expected

It's a rare case that the design sprint works perfectly and all your assumptions are validated. If this happens, you really should ask some questions: Did we push our assumptions hard enough? Did we dig deep enough into the problem? If so, then congratulations! This is a rare outcome, so enjoy the success. Depending on the fidelity of your prototype, you can use what you've created as the start of a product build.

The primary assumption the thoughtbot team was testing for with its Great Engagements prototype (discussed in Chapter 8) was whether a website could create an engaging, exciting, and emotional experience that would get people fantasizing about their wedding through images, storytelling, and high-quality information. This test was to determine if the team could engage and pull customers into the product and then more successfully introduce planning, communication tools, and premium services once customers move further down the engagement funnel. Through competitive analysis, the team also identified this emotional and aspirational experience as a means of differentiation in the market.

"The client supplied us with three interviewees (2 were done online, 1 in person; 1 was recently married). Though the dataset was limited due to the background and interest of those we interviewed, we gained some important insight to help us build a superior wedding planning product. People's complaints about competing wedding sites, such as The Knot, Wedding Wire, and Offbeat Bride, were about the lack of focus on those websites (too disorganized, too much information). They were most engaged by browsing things like wedding dresses, cakes, etc."

When shown the Great Engagements prototype, the users were engaged with a "Mad Libs" functionality, and large, eye-catching images that the team created.[2] The test subjects understood right away that the website is about venue discovery and their initial emotional reactions were that of excitement and inspiration, very much the reactions the team sought in order to validate the primary assumption. With these results, the team had the data necessary to further pursue concepts of immersive, inspirational, and aspirational exploration of venues in order to drive toward revenue-generating activities.

When Results Don't Match Your Expectations

Many users will include some surprises, as users often won't do what you expect them to. This is normal, so don't start freaking out yet. Sometimes most things work, but when some or all of a proposed solution is invalidated, you'll need to iterate. That's OK; this is actually cause for celebration. Keith Hooper runs his design sprints with the intent to fail everything. Taking a page from the bio-pharmaceutical and biotech world: fail early, because that means failing cheap. Think about the development of a pharmaceutical drug for a minute. It takes an average of 12 years and $350

---

2 Prototype site available at *http://greatengagements.herokuapp.com/.*

million to bring a drug from the laboratory to the pharmacy shelf.[3] The average cost for each phase of clinical trials: Phase I, $18.6 million; Phase II, $28.8 million; Phase III, $105.8 million.[4] This does not include the costs of preclinical and Phase 0. Nor does it include Phase IV. The earlier in the process you can fail, the less money you'll waste in developing the product. Digital products may not have the regimented approach that pharmaceuticals do, but they fail early and fail cheap. This can save you time and money as well. Remember Airtime? We don't either, but they spent $33 million on a product no one uses.[5]

As mentioned in Chapter 8, the outcome of the SMB Marketing Smarts design sprint was initially tough news. No one we tested wanted a mobile application for either phone or tablet as a way to help them with their email marketing and digital marketing activities. The action to download an entire mobile app specifically for help was not in their mental model when a search on Google resulted in a page (often on *constantcontact.com*) surfacing the answer they sought. However, this was only a four-day initiative. How much would it have cost the company if we proceeded to build that app, get it into the App Store, and then see only a handful of downloads and uses? That's a much worse outcome. It was a solution searching for a problem and we are glad that the design sprint shed light on this before any additional resources were spent on the project.

3 "New Drug Approval Process," *http://www.drugs.com/fda-approval-process.html.*

4 Erica Westly, "The Price of Winning FDA Approval," Fast Company, December/January 2010, *http://bit.ly/fastco-fda.*

5 Nicholas Carlson, "Absurdly Hyped Startup Airtime Has Officially Flopped and Top Execs are Fleeing," October 2, 2012, *http://bit.ly/airtime-flop.*

When You Still Have Questions

This is the most common case: questions remain. Some things worked, some things didn't. Do you know which and why? We'll discuss this in more depth in Chapter 10.

We mentioned Faze1 and how they stopped building products after doing a design sprint. The outcome of that particular design sprint fell under this category. The initial feedback was that they were somewhat onto a pain point, but something was not 100% right with the solution. Once the team members sat down and dug into the feedback, they realized the business model they were pursuing was flawed and would not produce the results they initially hoped for. They decided to stop building their product and spent more time with customers. This allowed them to rework their business model to something far more profitable.

In another example from thoughtbot, one design sprint invalidated two-thirds of a client's idea. The prototype showed metrics comparing users to others like them. When interviewed, users made it clear that other users' data did not matter to them. However, metrics comparing users to their own past behaviors was of great value to them. The team revised the prototype to show those metrics instead, and the participants showed greater interest and higher numbers on the "Scale of 1 to 10" question. With this pivot, the product proceeded and has been successful since.

Life is too short to build
something nobody wants.

– Ash Maurya, author of *Running Lean*

Takeaways

- Test with at least five people, up to eight if possible. Remember that someone will usually cancel.

- Test people individually; no group testing.

- Observe and take notes. Record if you can.

- Ask questions before guiding a stuck user to the next step.

- Use understandable language.

- End with a question to gauge whether you've created something users want.

- The results may not match your expectations.

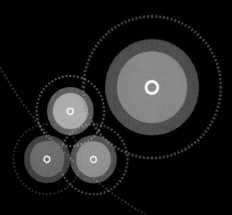

Chapter 10

After the Design Sprint: Capture, Iterate, and Continue

Congratulations, you've finished your design sprint! Now what? The answer to that question depends on how much validation you received during your interviews with users. It's time to reflect back on the entire initiative and see what worked, what didn't, and how to move forward. Don't limit yourself to considering the project itself; consider the entire design sprint process. We've mentioned repeatedly that this is a flexible framework and you can mold it to fit your needs. As we showed you in Chapter 3, there are plenty of ways to do this given your constraints. Did it work? What could you change to make it better?

A sprint summary document can vary widely depending on the project and the organization. We have some very detailed summary documents that are over 60 pages long. Others use a one-pager, executive summary style. The style and structure of your summary will depend on your team and organization's needs. Sure, you have the prototypes you created as artifacts, but those don't tell the whole story of the week, and this is the opportunity to do so. We take photographs of our walls, whiteboards, and Post-its (as you can see from the illustrations used in this book), and include them in our summary reports.

What Happens Next?

Capture and Document

Determine Next Steps

Continue the Practice

Capture and Document

Wrap-up documentation is helpful for the design sprint, whether you're a consulting firm or an in-house product team. These summary artifacts are excellent ways to get new team members up to speed on the project, and can also offer a historical snapshot, often answering questions such as "Why did we go in this direction?"

Here are three outline formats we have all used that might help you document your design sprint:

Example Format #1
Executive Summary
 Intro
Key Assumptions
 What we've learned
 Recommendations
Methods
 Research
 Assumptions
 Insights
 Ideation
 Prototype
Results
Conclusions and Recommendations
Appendix

Example Format #2
Executive Summary
Understand
Diverge
Converge
Build
Test
Conclusion
Appendix
 Assumption List
 Idea Parking Lot
 Sketches

Example Format #3
Where We Came From
Where We Arrived
What We Learned
Where to Go Next

For the design firm

Create a "capture document" that incorporates photographs of each day's activities. This includes all of the whiteboarding, Post-it notes, prototypes, discussion notes, and and anything else that was created during the day. The page layout looks like a photo album with pictures on one side and typed notes on the other. The notes often act as clarifications of the visual artifacts that were created. This document often will include several questions or identify gaps in our knowledge that need to be answered with further research.

The project team meets the day after the second session for a final debrief and discussion on scope. This normally takes about an hour to clarify scope, scheduling, and budget. The product manager then writes up the statement of work (SOW) and master services agreement (MSA) and sends it over to the client for approval. If this is approved, the SOW becomes the contract to start the design and development of the product.

For the product team within an organization

The design sprint will give direction to where the product team needs to go next by arming a team with qualitative customer evidence of where the product directions should go. What we frequently see happen is the teams will incorporate design directions into their product workflows or even define a new road map. The Constant Contact team created a mechanism called a "Jump Start" that incorporates the lean-startup "Build-Measure-Learn" ethos to further refine a product's features and experience. It's a hypothesis-driven approach that continues the iterative design process. Each "Jump Start" is usually one week long, and not as intense as a design sprint. Sometimes a prototype is the manner in which the hypothesis will be tested and sometimes it is not. It depends on what's necessary to learn. It could be a market survey, a pricing survey, competitive analysis, or something else entirely so long as it helps you gain clarity.

Determine Next Steps

The design sprint cannot answer every question and provide a flawless road map, but it can set a strong foundation for forward direction. Since the inception of design sprints as an accepted methodology for solving product problems, there have been thousands of sprints and prototypes. Doing a design sprint won't always guarantee a product launch, but it will help ensure that a poorly conceived product idea will not survive. In the cases where a design makes it through validation, the process may even generate a design and development road map.

As we've mentioned, the design sprint is a great springboard that will accelerate the learning of the team as well as the alignment on which direction a product can take.

Continue the Practice

Incorporating design sprints as part of your standard workflow is a great practice, and although there will be challenges, you'll find you'll deliver higher quality products, features, and experiences to the market.

Make Design Sprints Commonplace

Designers sometimes struggle with Agile, but this methodology of doing continuous discovery, or continuous design, requires buy-in from the entire organization. It's easier to get people aligned upfront and then continuously repeat this process like a discipline, like a kata. We liken the concept of *Shu Ha Ri,* a Japanese martial art concept used to describe the stages of learning through mastery, when considering the adoption of this approach to an organization. In recent years, it has been abstracted and applied to the cycle of learning in general. Martin Fowler, Alistair Cockburn, and many others have written about the use and application of *Shu Ha Ri* in Agile organizations.

Fowler defines *Shu Ha Ri* as follows:

Shu – *In this beginning stage the student follows the teachings of one master precisely. He concentrates on how to do the task, without worrying too much about the underlying theory. If there are multiple variations on how to do the task, he concentrates on just the one way his master teaches him.*

Ha – *At this point the student begins to branch out. With the basic practices working he now starts to learn the underlying principles and theory behind the technique. He also starts learning from other masters and integrates that learning into his practice.*

Ri – *Now the student isn't learning from other people, but from his own practice. He creates his own approaches and adapts what he's learned to his own particular circumstances.*

Consider this from an organizational standpoint. In *Shu*, the organization is learning, sticking to the processes defined. Once it starts breaking the methodology apart, it is in *Ha* and after years of making the methodology its own, adjusting to the particular organization needs, it will then become *Ri*, where it is a part of the embedded culture and not specifically thought of in terms of framework or process. If you are just starting to incorporate design sprints into your organization, *Shu Ha Ri* may be a good lens to view the journey. While a design sprint is short, the road to organization-wide adoption is long. It took C. Todd over two years and dozens of design sprints to reach an inflection point of a broader-scale adoption at Constant Contact, and there's still a long way to go to fully integrate the practice across the enterprise. Your mileage may vary, so keep at it!

It's in Your Hands

We hope this book has given you a solid understanding for how to run a design sprint with your team. As we have mentioned, this process is quite flexible. We have provided a fairly prescriptive approach, but each of us has done design sprints that diverge (pun intended) from what we prescribe here. We are constantly experimenting and evolving our own design sprint practices, and we encourage you to as well. We've shared stories from our colleagues so that you can see the different approaches taken to adapt to varying organizational constraints. The basic ethos is there: a cathartic timeboxed design cycle driven by assumptions and bookended with customer input and feedback.

Takeaways

- Get together at the end of the sprint to review your assumptions and findings.

- Create some kind of capture document as an artifact to share with colleagues and/or clients.

- If most things worked, next steps can include tuning the prototype and preparing to start work on your product or service.

- If some things worked but there are large questions, iterate with a smaller design sprint to get them resolved.

- If nothing worked, start over—maybe with another design sprint!

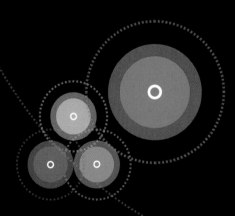

Image Credits

Index